Government Policy
toward
Open Source Software

Government Policy toward Open Source Software

Robert W. Hahn
editor

AEI-Brookings Joint Center for Regulatory Studies

WASHINGTON, D. C.

2002

Government Policy toward Open Source Software may be ordered from:

Brookings Institution Press
1775 Massachusetts Avenue, N.W.
Washington, D.C. 20036
Tel.: 1-800-275-1447 or (202) 797-6258
Fax: (202) 797-6004
www.brookings.edu

QA
76.76
° S46
G 68
2002

Library of Congress Cataloging-in-Publication data

Government policy toward open source software / Robert W. Hahn, editor.
    p.   cm.
Includes bibliographical references.
    ISBN 0-8157-3393-3
    1. Open source software—Government policy. 2. Free computer software—Government policy. I. Hahn, Robert William. II. AEI-Brookings Joint Center for Regulatory Studies.

QA76.76.S46 G68 2002
005.3—dc21   2002015514

9 8 7 6 5 4 3 2 1

The paper used in this publication meets minimum requirements of the American National Standard for Information Sciences—Permanence of Paper for Printed Library Materials: ANSI Z39.48-1992.

Typeset in Berkeley

Composition by Cynthia Stock
Silver Spring, Maryland

Printed by Edwards Brothers
Lillington, North Carolina

Foreword

This volume, commissioned by the AEI-Brookings Joint Center for Regulatory Studies, is one in a series that contributes to the ongoing debate over the regulation of high-technology industries—and, in particular, the information technology industry. The Joint Center is focusing on this debate because its outcome could have huge ramifications for the growth of the economy and the well-being of consumers.

We invited four leading experts to address the policy issues associated with what has come to be known as "open source" software. Open source software, such as the Linux computer operating system, is usually available without charge. Moreover, in contrast to most proprietary software, such as the Windows operating system, individuals can modify it because they have access to the underlying source code written in widely understood programming languages.

The book addresses several issues related to open source software, including the role for government subsidies for research and development, government procurement policy, and patent policy. The contributors to this volume offer diverse views on a phenomenon that has become a touchstone for controversy in the information technology business.

Our goal is to highlight the fundamental areas of agreement and disagreement on government policy toward open source software. More generally, we hope that this volume will illuminate the issues involved in assessing the appropriate scope for government intervention in the information technology industry.

The views expressed here are those of the authors and should not be attributed to the trustees, officers, or staff members of the American Enterprise Institute or the Brookings Institution.

ROBERT W. HAHN
ROBERT E. LITAN
AEI-Brookings Joint Center for Regulatory Studies

Contents

1

Government Policy toward Open Source Software: An Overview

Robert W. Hahn

This chapter provides a brief overview of policy issues associated with open source software and offers an economic framework for thinking about these issues. It includes a thumbnail sketch of the main points made by each of the contributors, highlighting areas of agreement and conflict on key policy questions.

This book examines the impact of government policy on open source software. "Open source" refers to access to the source code, written in a programming language, that constitutes a working software program. With open source software, users and others can read the code and change it to suit their needs.[1]

Several open source software programs and their relatives, free software programs, are widely used today.[2] The best known is the computer operating system Linux.[3] To date, Linux has been most successful as an operating system for servers—computers on a network used for tasks such as managing printers, storing files, and sending web pages to users—but could expand to the desktop (PC) market in the future. Other examples of widely embraced open source products include Sendmail (an email server program), Apache (a web server program), and StarOffice (a business applications suite).[4] And acceptance is growing: Linux gained enough use as a server operating system market in 2001 to be included in industry tracking studies.[5]

Physically, open source software and other software look the same. If you made copies of two operating systems—say, Linux and Windows—and put them on new CDs, you couldn't tell the difference unless they were labeled. Essentially, they both consist of binary code, strings of ones and zeros. Yet the way in which Linux and Windows were created is totally different. And the way in which they can be legally modified is totally different.

Linux comes out of the "open source" tradition, while Windows is proprietary. If you obtain a copy of Linux, the source code comes as part of the package. By contrast, access to the source code for Windows is tightly restricted and provided separately to Microsoft business partners on a "need to know" basis. Not surprisingly, then, the process by which open source and proprietary closed source software is created comes from very different—and sometimes conflicting—traditions.

On the one hand, programmers often flourish as part of communities that prize cooperation and openness. Status within the community is largely derived from showing how good one is at programming—which requires showing off the source code— and how committed one is to furthering the collective effort— which requires providing source code for others to work from.[6] The Internet made it far easier to develop software this way and is generally viewed as the catalyst to the open source boom.

But open source can pay off on the demand side, too. Some users of software greatly value the option "to look under the hood" and to have the ability to make changes. Access to source code, for example, makes it possible for information technology professionals who maintain computer networks to tailor generic software to their specific needs and to debug software on the fly. Indeed, one reason the Linux operating system for server computers has been so popular is that it gives sophisticated users great flexibility and reduces their dependence on software vendors.

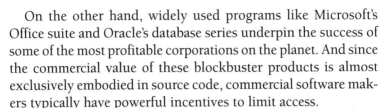

On the other hand, widely used programs like Microsoft's Office suite and Oracle's database series underpin the success of some of the most profitable corporations on the planet. And since the commercial value of these blockbuster products is almost exclusively embodied in source code, commercial software makers typically have powerful incentives to limit access.

Like other businesses relying on intellectual property, they use patents and copyrights to safeguard the value of their property. Unlike most others, however, software companies' first and strongest line of defense is secrecy.[7] It may be relatively easy to copy a CD containing a compiled version of Windows that is ready to bring a PC to life. But that copy would not provide any clues to the design of the underlying source code and thus would be of little or no help in cloning Windows—even to a highly experienced programmer.

For many software users, the absence of source code is not a drawback. While open source software is often geared toward information technology specialists, to whom the availability of source code can be a real asset, proprietary software is often aimed at less sophisticated users. Most of the people who use Windows on their PCs—either at work or at home—would not know what to do with source code even if they had access to it. These users are more concerned about standard features and ease of use than they are about customization. As a result, proprietary software developers spend considerably more resources on documentation, customer support, and product training than do open source providers. Proprietary vendors also expend more effort researching what average users want through surveys and such, rather than relying on early product testers and fellow software developers' opinions.

Open source software can coexist with commercial software in market niches where flexibility is paramount and communal development works well. In others, where ease of use or customer support and training are more important and financial incentives spur innovation, commercial software may dominate.

But the availability of both open source and proprietary software in the same market can create tensions. For example, some

open source software is licensed under terms that make it difficult for the software to coexist with commercial software. Indeed, the Free Software Foundation apparently sees the
destruction of incentives to produce software under the conventional commercial model as a prime objective. Its General Public
License (GPL) requires that any modifications or additions to
GPL-licensed software also be licensed under the same terms,
making it difficult for developers to profit financially from distributing this software.[8]

The key features of the GPL, which is sometimes called
"viral" because its integration with other code automatically
transforms the integrated version into GPL code, may have important economic implications. For example, while Sun Microsystems was able to create a commercial hit—with early versions
of the Solaris operating system—from the Berkeley Software
Distribution (BSD)-licensed Unix operating system source code,
no one will ever replicate that feat with Linux. Any software
derived from GPL-licensed Linux must be distributed with an
accessible copy of the source code, and the rights to use any
modifications in the source code must be free to all, thereby
making it very difficult to profit from using Linux code as part
of proprietary software.

Arguably more important, some governments have expressly
tilted the playing field toward open source software, subsidizing
its production and use. Instead of choosing software based on
its merits—reliability, security, ease of use, and so on—these
governments favor open source as a matter of policy. For instance, Singapore is offering tax breaks to companies that use
the open source Linux operating system instead of commercial
alternatives like Windows. This and other examples of government support of open source software around the world are
shown on table 1-1.

In addition to the handful of measures that have already passed
in Brazil, Germany, and Singapore, many more governments
worldwide have open source proposals pending, and the European Parliament has called on member nations to promote the
use of open source software whenever practical. Table 1-2 lists

Table 1-1. Existing Government Support of Open Source
Software around the World

Country	Proposal	Date adopted
Asia		
Singapore	Government agency (the EDB) charged with planning and executing strategies to boost the Singapore economy offered temporary tax reductions and financial grants to fund Linux-related projects.	2001
Europe		
Germany	Compensation legislation requiring that right holders (such as copyrights holders) generally may not waive in advance their rights to adequate compensation for use of their works. An exception inserted at the request of open source lobbyists permits waiver of this right if the right holder grants rights to simple use of the work to the general public.	January 2002
	Bundestag mandated a new IT environment: Linux on servers, Windows on desktops.	March 2002
	Government-IBM agreement that offers German government offices discounts on IBM machines with preinstalled Linux provided by German Linux distributor SuSE.	June 2002
Latin America		
Brazil	Legislation mandating open source software be given preference in municipal governments of Recife, Campinas, Solonopole, Amparo, Sao Carlos, and Porto Alegre.	2001

Sources: The German compensation bill text is available at www.bundestag.de/aktuell/ bp/2002/bp0201/0201028.html (German; August 21, 2002); for the Bundestag's adoption of the new IT environment, see www.heise.de/newsticker/data/anw-14.03.02-012/ (German; August 21, 2002). For legislation in Recife, see www. pernambuco.com/tecnologia/ arquivo/softlivre1.html (Portuguese; August 21, 2002); for Campinas, see www.aful. org/politique/perou/english/referencias.html (August 21, 2002); for Solonopole, see www.solonopole.ce.gov.br/leis/614-2001.htm (Portuguese; August 21, 2002); for Amparo, see www.cipsgapf.hpg.ig.com.br/projetos/dimas_marchi.htm (Portuguese; August 21, 2002); for Sao Carlos, see www.softwarelivre.rs.gov.br/index.php?menu= maisnoticias&codigonoticia=1009655036 (Portuguese; August 21, 2002); and for Porto Alegre, see www.seprors.com.br/swlivre.htm (Portuguese; August 21, 2002). For a general overview of global proposals, see www.infoworld.com/articles/hn/xml/02/06/12/ 020612hnossnapshot.xml (August 21, 2002).

Table 1-2. Pending Legislation on Open Source Software
around the World

Country	Proposal	Date proposed/ last action
Europe		
France	Parliamentary bill forbidding government-related institutions to use anything but open source software.	December 1999
Italy	Bills mandating an open source software preference in all governmental offices.	February 2002 and March 2002
Spain	Bill requiring regional governments to prefer and promote open source products.	May 2002
	Bill submitted to the Catalan parliament mandating an open source preference in all regional administrative bodies.	May 2002
	Motion by the Izquierda Unida Party urging the Senate to ensure that all public administration websites, documents, and software are Linux-compatible.	July 2001
Latin America		
Argentina	Bill mandating use of open source software by all provincial administrations in the Buenos Aires province.	June 2002
	Bill mandating all governmental offices to use "free software."	September 2000
Brazil	Legislative proposals mandating preference for open source software in all governmental offices.	1999, 2000, 2001
Peru	Legislative proposals mandating preference for open source software in all governmental offices.	March 2002 and April 2002

Sources: For the parliamentary bill in France, see www.senat.fr/leg/pp199-117.html
(French; August 21, 2002); for the bills in Italy, see www.senato.it/leg/14/bgt/schede/
ddliter/16976.htm (Italian; August 21, 2002); for the parliamentary bill in Spain, see
www.senado.es/legis7/publicaciones/pdf/congreso/bocg/b0244-1.pdf (Spanish; August 21,
2002); for the bill submitted to the Catalan Parliament, see www.hispalinux.es/
modules.php?op=modload&name=sections&file=index&req=viewarticle&artid=49
(Spanish; August 21, 2002); and for the motion by the Izquierda Unida Party, see
www.senado.es/legis7/publicaciones/html/textos/i0259.html#9 (Spanish; August 21, 2002).
For the bill in the Buenos Aires province, the proposal in Cordoba, and the bill mandat-
ing all governmental offices to use "free software" in Argentina, see www.grulic.org.ar
(Spanish; August 21, 2002) and www.aful.org/politique/perou/english/referencias.html
(August 21, 2002). For the legislative proposals in Brazil, see www.camara.gov.br/internet/
sileg/prop_detalhe.asp?id=17879, www.camara.gov.br/internet/sileg/prop_detalhe.
asp?id=19028, and www.camara.gov.br/internet/sileg/prop_detalhe.asp?id=26688 (Portuguese; August 21, 2002). For the legislative proposals in Peru, see www.gnu.org.pe/
proley4.html and www.gnu.org.pe/proley3.html (Spanish; August 21, 2002).

regulations that are still working their way through the legislative process.[9]

To economists, the market itself seems a natural place to resolve the conflict between diverging models for developing and distributing software. But this is only true if the market for software works reasonably well to benefit consumers. If, however, there is a significant "market failure," some kind of government intervention may be justified. In the case of software, such failures could arise either on the demand side or the supply side—if either buyers or sellers do not capture the full value of the product.[10]

Even if there were a significant market failure, however, government intervention may not be justified on economic grounds. A reasonable economic standard for government intervention is when the benefits of such intervention are likely to outweigh the costs by a substantial margin.[11]

Is the software market characterized by a significant market failure? Or is the movement to promote open source an ironic throwback to an era in which government was widely seen as the appropriate manager of technological change? And what, if any, government intervention is needed?

The following chapters offer the reader diverse views on government policy toward open source software by four leading experts in the field. In chapter 2 James Bessen argues that open source software meets specialized needs not met by either packaged or customized proprietary software. He contends that open source extends the software market by addressing market failures associated with incomplete contracts and asymmetric information. To encourage open source software development, he argues, the government should remove the impediments it has imposed in the form of software patents, which tilt the market in favor of proprietary developers.

In chapter 3 David Evans argues that there is no market failure in the provision of software and therefore no need for government remediation. On the contrary, the government should act like a business in making its own software investment decisions, evaluating software on its merits as a product rather than attempting to promote a particular kind of software. Moreover, if the government decides to support open source through research and development funding, it should remain consistent with its approach in other fields and help to promote the commercialization of the resulting research by licensing software on terms that are less restrictive than those imposed by the GPL.

In chapter 4 Lawrence Lessig argues that the government has broader interests in software than private companies, including an interest in achieving and maintaining an open platform. As Lessig explains, "Between two systems for producing a public good, one that releases the information produced by that good freely and one that does not, all things being equal, public policy should favor free access."[12] Thus a "neutral" government could still come out in favor of open source software.

In the final chapter, Bradford Smith posits that the marketplace, rather than the policy arena, creates the best combination of incentives and flexibility to ensure that software continues to satisfy consumer needs. He argues that government policies favoring open source over proprietary software would disrupt the software "ecosystem." Instead, government could play a role in promoting software research under licensing terms that allow the results to be commercialized.

While there are clear differences of opinion among these experts, there are also some areas of agreement. Table 1-3 provides a glimpse of where they stand on key policy questions.

The first row of the table examines whether the author explicitly identifies a significant market failure in the development or production of software. As noted above, economists generally think it is important to identify such a failure before considering government intervention in a market. Interestingly, only one of the authors identifies a significant market failure in the provision of open source software. Yet several of the authors do think significant government policy interventions should be implemented or considered.

The second row in the table examines the author's view on subsidies for open source software. None explicitly supports direct subsidies for open source software.

Table 1-3. Viewpoints on Government Policy toward Open Source Software

Issue	James Bessen	David Evans	Lawrence Lessig	Bradford Smith
1. Identifies a significant market failure in the development or production of open source software.	*No, but:* notes that open source solves a market failure in software provision by overcoming imperfect contracts and information asymmetry.	*No:* the software industry has performed extremely well in terms of production and innovation without any government intervention.	*Yes, but:* open source developers cannot fully capture the value of their work, but this does not necessarily destroy the incentive to innovate.	*No:* there is currently no market failure in software.
2. Argues for direct government subsidies for open source.	*No:* where the government has intervened (in patents), it has created a market failure.	*No:* the government should not be in the position to pick industry winners.	*No:* the government should be neutral but careful to address its own interests.	*No:* only the market-place can satisfy actual market needs.
3. Believes open source and proprietary software both have important roles to play.	*Yes:* open source software extends the market.	*Yes:* the open source method is an important organizational innovation.	*Yes:* both forms of software production should compete in the market.	*Yes:* both open source and commercial software are integral parts of the software ecosystem.
4. Argues that government should make software procurement based on benefit-cost framework similar to a profit-maximizing firm.	*Yes:* products should be considered on their merits for the project at hand.	*Yes:* governments ought to pick the best products for their own internal needs.	*Yes, but:* the government has a greater interest in externalizing benefits such as an open platform.	*Not addressed.*
5. Suggests government should encourage firms to commercialize research and development by not permitting GPL or "viral" license to be used in government-funded research.	*Not addressed.*	*Yes:* governments should ensure that the results of publicly funded research are not subject to licensing restrictions.	*No:* no general rule can be asserted. Sometimes it will make sense for the government to support GPL projects.	*Yes:* governments can help promote innovation through research and development and should facilitate commercialization of the resulting research.
6. Suggests government should change patent policy to allow open source to be more competitive.	*Yes:* Congress could restore subject matter limitations on patents and strict standards on patent quality.	*No, but:* might strike a better balance between protection and innovation if software patent standards were tougher and patent lives shorter.	*Yes:* a system with software patents is biased against open source and free software.	*Not addressed.*

The third row of the table shows that all authors believe that open source and proprietary software have important roles to play in the market. Indeed, both sources of software are widely used, though it is fair to conclude that proprietary software plays a dominant role at this point. In chapters 3 and 5, respectively, Evans and Smith discuss the remarkable growth that has occurred in proprietary software. In chapter 2, however, Bessen notes that a growing number of users are turning to open source, especially for custom software projects.

The question of the government's role in procurement of software is addressed in the fourth row. All three authors who address the issue argue that the government should base its purchasing decisions for software on criteria similar to those used by private firms—that is, on narrow economic grounds. Lessig notes the importance of considering the value derived from standardization and openness when the government makes its purchasing decisions. I also think a private firm would want to consider such values.[13]

Some scholars and some firms have argued that the government should not fund research that is licensed under the GPL or similar "viral" licenses. They note that such funding could dampen innovation by deterring private firms from using the results in new services or products because of the peculiar nature of viral software.[14] This issue is of more than theoretical interest. The U.S. government is already licensing software this way. For example, software underwritten by NASA and by the Sandia National Laboratories has already been distributed under the GPL. The fifth row in table 1-3 summarizes the views of the authors on this issue: Evans and Smith argue against such funding, but Lessig argues that it may sometimes make sense for the government to support GPL projects.

The final row in the table shows the authors' views on changing patent law to promote innovation in software. There seems to be a consensus among the three authors who address the issue that some change would be useful. Bessen and Lessig argue that patent law is currently biased against open source software, and they favor stricter standards for patents. Evans also believes there may be an argument for stricter standards because it would generally help software innovation. This is an area that would benefit greatly from more empirical research.

This book is meant to contribute to the debate on open source policy. At this point, I think it is fair to say that a strong quantitative case has not been made for government intervention in this market. This is perhaps why none of the experts here favors direct government subsidies for open source. At the same time, there may be good economic reasons for changing aspects of government policy toward software in areas ranging from procurement to patents. This book is aimed at shedding light on such policy issues as well as on broader aspects in the debate over open source software.

2

What Good Is Free Software?

James Bessen

When you use the World Wide Web, it is likely that the web pages are sent to you by software that was developed by unpaid volunteers. The majority of web servers on the public Internet use an open source software program called Apache.[1] This free product was developed by a loosely organized team of hundreds of programmers and thousands of other people reporting bugs or requesting enhancements, none of whom were paid by the Apache group for their efforts.[2] Yet Apache competes successfully with well-funded commercial products developed by Microsoft, Sun, and other companies.

This seems paradoxical in an age when conventional wisdom holds that markets driven purely by private interest best serve collective needs. But I argue here that the paradox has a straightforward explanation. Although some developers of open source software are indeed motivated by altruism, many are members of communities that benefit from the development of software along very flexible lines. In particular, firms driven by the conventional profit motive find open source software valuable because it allows them to meet their specific idiosyncratic needs—needs not easily met with standardized software products. I argue that for complex software products these unmet needs constitute a major source of demand, providing a robust long-term economic foundation for open source software.

In a sense, open source provision is an *extension* of the market, not an alternative. Private agents meet private needs. As I explain below, instead of providing software in exchange for money, open source developers provide software in exchange for a (sometimes informal) promise to improve the product and return the fruits of their invention to the community. Government support is thus not necessary to sustain open source development. However, I argue that the U.S. government is nonetheless intervening in this market in a very different way, ironically sabotaging the otherwise healthy open source movement.

Over the last two decades, the courts have radically changed the legal protection of the ideas embodied in software, making it much easier to obtain patents, even for rather obvious ideas. The courts made these changes despite a high level of innovation in the software industry and without any evidence that these patents would improve (or had improved) the pace of innovation. In response, large firms have acquired thousands of patents in order to strategically block competitors. The resulting "patent thickets" threaten the ability of open source developers to improve software and may thus undermine this important source of innovation in the future.

This chapter offers two contributions. First, it presents an economic rationale for the participation of for-profit enterprises in open source development of complex products.[3] Much of the previous economics research on open source has focused on the participation of individual users who are also programmers (user-developers) with simple needs. For example, Josh Lerner and Jean Tirole attribute much individual motivation to reputation building, while Justin Johnson and Jennifer Kuan model individual user-developers with common needs but heterogeneous valuations and abilities.[4] Second, this chapter presents the argument that changes in patent regulation, in particular those encouraging the growth of patent thickets, threaten the development of open source software.

The discussion begins with a description of open source software and free software, followed by a comparison of these forms to proprietary provision of software. In subsequent sections, I argue that open source does not generally require government financial support, and I briefly consider government procurement policies with this reality in mind. The chapter concludes with an analysis of the effects of patents on open source, with recommendations for changes in patent policy.

Free and Open Source Software

Since the early days of computing, users have shared computer code. Many important early programs, including many developed with government funding, were freely passed around. In the 1950s and 1960s, proprietary software consisted of limited applications that were almost entirely sold bundled with computer hardware. Little packaged software was sold until the 1970s, when IBM was challenged by private and government lawsuits to unbundle and when minicomputers came into wide use.[5]

In the mid-1980s a new, more formalized model for sharing software code emerged. The computer scientist Richard Stallman, concerned about limits on his ability to access, modify, and improve software, started the free software movement.[6] He developed the GNU General Public License (GPL) for software programs. Under the GPL the user obtains free access to the software code and agrees that any redistribution of the code will also be freely available, including any modifications the user makes to the code.

Free software gained momentum during the mid-1990s, with the emergence of the Internet. Developers such as Linus Torvalds, the initial creator of Linux, pioneered new organizational schemes that made it possible for hundreds of volunteer programmers to participate in joint software development over the Internet. Out of this broad participation arose the open source movement, which includes software developed under the GPL as well as other license agreements.

It is helpful to define some terms. First, note that there are two senses in which free software is free: it has zero direct cost to the user, and it provides the freedom to modify the software. Stallman emphasizes the latter usage. Free software, he explains, is "free as in 'free speech,' not as in 'free beer.'"[7] This distinction is important for two reasons. First, free software is not at all the same as "freeware," which is zero-price software with closed source code that is often provided as a trial product. Second, it is highly misleading to view the main economic attribute of free software as its price. As is well known, the total cost of installing a software program includes many other costs; even with proprietary software, the price of the software is usually only a modest portion of the total user cost.[8] Also, as I explain below, large economic benefits arise from the freedom to modify the source code.

Open source software includes free software subject to the GPL, but it also includes other license agreements that permit access to the source code. Some of these license agreements permit the user to incorporate free code into proprietary, closed source products. For example, versions of open source Unix have been incorporated into closed source operating systems under non-GPL licenses.

Note, however, that for many products, public code is rarely included in proprietary products even when the license allows this. That is particularly true for dynamically improving products, in contrast to mature products such as standard Unix. First, open source developers are not motivated to improve software if they suspect it will be converted to a proprietary product. Second, and perhaps more important, creating proprietary software from open source code is often difficult because open source software typically changes rapidly. One of the key aspects of open source products such as Apache is that large numbers of modifications, improvements, and bug fixes are made and rapidly incorporated into new releases. Any private modifications would have to be continually re-integrated into new releases at significant cost. So although someone could legally use the Apache code to produce a customized closed source product, this has not been done. Firms offering proprietary web servers develop their own code from scratch.

Here I use the term "open source" to include free software distributed under the GPL as well as software distributed under other licenses.

To understand the nature of open source software, it is necessary to dispel some misunderstandings. Reading the business press, one might conclude that open source software is a marginal, transitory activity that lacks the solid economic rationale of proprietary software. Open source software is portrayed as the province of young idealists, graduate students, and teenage hackers rather than the serious business of corporate management information systems (MIS) departments with mission-critical computer systems to keep online. Others suggest open source is something of a fad.[9] Perhaps most important, open source programmers are presumed to be motivated by altruism rather than by traditional profit motives—as the *Economist* tells us, "for love, not money."[10]

This last point, in particular, reinforces the occupational prejudices of economists. They tend to think in terms of standardized commodities because they have had considerable success explaining markets for standardized proprietary commodities. They naturally view Microsoft Office as the ideal sort of software, while Microsoft is frequently viewed as the prototypical software enterprise. Furthermore, they have a lot of experience suggesting that traditional proprietary incentives are highly efficient means of providing standardized commodities.

Consequently, economists, if not outright skeptical about open source, tend to view it as a puzzle to be explained. Clearly, it is possible for a bunch of idealistic programmers to write a lot of code, but staying power requires more than just altruism.

The pundits said many of the same things about the PC and PC software twenty years ago. PC software was written by young idealists who supposedly weren't up to the task of writing serious corporate software. After all, a college dropout (Gates at Microsoft) and a Transcendental Meditation instructor (Kapor at Lotus) ran the leading PC software companies. But, of course, new software is usually written by people who do not have a large vested interest in old software.

In reality, open source software has become serious business. IBM is investing a billion dollars in open source projects, and many other large companies are joining in, too. By the same token, some open source products have achieved a high degree of success, such as the Apache web server, which holds a 64 percent share of active, publicly accessible web servers.[11] A study at the University of Wisconsin found open source UNIX operating systems were more reliable than more mature commercial products, and a study at Berkeley found superior debugging among open source software projects.[12] In addition, industry surveys have found a higher degree of customer satisfaction among open source users.[13] Note, too, that open source programmers are not primarily teenage hackers—a recent survey found that the average active participant had ten years of programming experience.[14]

It is true that most open source products are directed at technically sophisticated users, and many are not very "user friendly." Some people argue that this is no accident: open source coders are unlikely to develop programs for less sophisticated users.[15] However, the current technical bias may just be a result of the newness of the software. Early PC and minicomputer software was hardly user-friendly—Microsoft took over a decade to deliver products easily grasped by the untutored. And there are important signs of ongoing progress. Graphical user interfaces (from KDE and Gnome) for the GNU/Linux operating system are now widely used.[16] And according to some reviewers, the recently released open source Mozilla web browser can meet or beat Microsoft's Internet Explorer for usability.[17] Thus it is simply too soon to tell whether open source is in any fundamental way limited in its ability to address the needs of less technical users.[18]

Not only has open source software achieved some important successes, it also appears to be gaining momentum and improving rapidly. The number of developers registered at SourceForge, a popular website for open source participants, continues to grow rapidly and now exceeds 400,000.[19] The software they produce has grown in sophistication and features. For example, the Apache program was initially used for small, individual web servers. Large websites that handled tens of thousands of users at once needed industrial strength "application servers," such as Weblogic from BEA. Now, however, open source products such as Tomcat and Jboss are moving into that territory.[20]

Finally, it is simply not true that most open source developers are solely motivated by altruism. A recent survey by the Boston Consulting Group found a wide variety of motives.[21] Some developers get involved with open source projects to learn cutting edge technology. For this reason, open source programs are now widely used in university computer science courses. Others seek a sense of community in participating in open source projects. Yet others hope to build their reputation through involvement that advances their careers.[22] Finally, in many cases, participation in open source development permits individuals and firms to obtain software that is customized to their particular needs.

All of these motives are important. I will focus on the last one—the ability to customize software for in-house needs—because I see this incentive as a critical reason why firms (and not just individual programmers) want to participate in open source development and why a growing share of software is likely to be developed with open source code. Indeed, as I elaborate below, the need for customized software may drive firms to open source development to improve the bottom line. Thus it is a false dichotomy to pose open source and proprietary development as a contrast between altruism and private incentives.

Software and Markets

A large economics literature convincingly argues that markets are efficient mechanisms for meeting many private needs. Markets can provide the strongest incentives for private agents to undertake the investments necessary to make the commodities that best meet the demand. For example, consider standardized commodities in large markets. It may be too expensive for each consumer to produce the commodity for his or her own needs.

Figure 2-1. Packaged Software Share of Investment, 1962–98

Percent

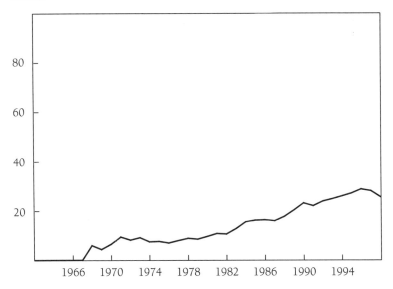

Source: Data from Robert Parker and Bruce Grimm, "Recognition of Business and Government Expenditures for Software as Investment: Methodology and Quantitative Impacts, 1959–98," report presented at the meeting of the Bureau of Economic Analysis, May 5, 2000 (www.bea.doc.gov/bea/papers/software.pdf [August 2002]).

The market serves to aggregate demand for a standardized product from many different consumers. Then a firm can make profits that are sufficient to cover production and development costs. But most software is not a standardized commodity. Although Microsoft is often viewed as the prototypical software firm, most software is not packaged software. Indeed, as figure 2-1 illustrates, packaged software has never accounted for more than a third of software investment. The majority of software produced is either self-developed or custom. This is quite different from typical commodities, and for this reason, arguments grounded in analysis of typical commodities need to be examined carefully. The ability to tailor programs to meet specific needs is an essential characteristic of software. This is what is "soft" in software, and this is why software-hardware systems are economically advantageous in so many applications.

The customizability of this good affects the nature of the product and the nature of the market. Standardized software packages are, at best, a compromise. Attempting to meet as large a set of individual consumer's needs as possible, standardized packages cram in as many features as is feasible. This is why successful products so often suffer from feature "bloat."[23] Standardized packages also frequently have "macro extensions"— tools included in word processor, spreadsheet, or other applications that allow consumers to customize the packages to a limited degree with a programming language. But the cost of debugging ultimately limits the ability of standardized products to meet highly disparate needs. As products accumulate features, their code becomes much more complex, and debugging costs grow exponentially.[24] Thus developers of standardized products face a trade-off between feature richness and product quality and reliability.[25] Restricting features limits the ability of standardized products to meet the needs of software consumers. Hence, packaged software represents only a minority of software investment.

Custom software and contract programming provide an alternative proprietary means for meeting the needs of individual consumers. But customization will not, in general, meet the needs of all consumers for two well-understood reasons. First, as anyone who has negotiated a custom programming contract knows, it is very difficult to specify the contract. This is because the only complete specification of all the software features and its behavior under all circumstances is the software code itself.

In effect, consumers cannot specify what they want the software to do in all circumstances until they actually have the software in hand. Any software contract is thus what economists call an incomplete contract. When contracts are incomplete, many consumers will not have their needs met by proprietary providers. Second, negotiations over custom contracts also suffer from asymmetric information.[26] That is, the developer does not know how much value the consumer places on the product and therefore does not know what to charge. With standardized commodities, market demand is revealed through many transactions. But with a custom product, developers cannot obtain this information without a costly bilateral bargaining process. As a result, a developer may not offer a custom contract, even though a contract on terms that are profitable would be accepted. Alternatively, the developer may overreach and ask for too much, leading the consumer to reject the offer.

Incomplete contracts and asymmetric information result in some degree of market failure.[27] That is, some consumers are not served even though their needs could be met with profitable contracts. Note, however, that such market imperfections cannot be corrected by direct government intervention—the government is in no better position to design or negotiate contracts than private software developers.

But open source development may finesse these problems by allowing consumers to customize products themselves. Open source means, roughly, that consumers are provided with 99 percent of their desired product in a form that allows some of them to tailor the remaining 1 percent to their own needs. When the consumer *is* the developer, problems of specification or valuation are easily resolved.

The open source developer makes the desired enhancements or fixes and then, under the most common licenses, submits them back to the open source project. They are then incorporated into future releases and improve the value of the product for other consumers who may have similar needs. This works for enhancements to product features, for entirely new features, and for bug fixes. Because so many active user-developers become involved, the quality, reliability, and overall value of the product can grow quite rapidly.

Moreover, many consumers of software who aren't developers have the same needs as some of the user-developers.[28] In these cases, the feature-rich products and the large variety of customized add-on modules produced by open source user-developers benefit many nondevelopers as well.

The Apache web server illustrates the importance of customization and feature enhancement for open source users. In one survey regarding security features, 19 percent of the firms using Apache had modified the code to these ends, and another 33 percent customized the product by incorporating add-on security modules available from third parties.[29] Open source code facilitates the provision of add-on modules, and over 300 of these have been developed for Apache.[30] Many are quite popular: sixteen add-ons have at least 1 percent market share, and one (PHP) has 45 percent market share.[31] Moreover, many private enhancements are shared with the community and incorporated in new versions of the product. During the first three years of Apache, 388 developers contributed 6,092 enhancements and fixed 695 bugs.[32] This far exceeds the rate of feature enhancement for comparable commercial products.[33]

The breadth and dynamism of this participation demonstrate the degree to which open source software extends the market. Apache is used primarily by firms, not by individuals. So firms choose to customize their software and then choose to contribute these modifications back to the Apache group or to make them available as add-ons. Although personal motivations such as altruism, learning, community participation, and reputation all contribute to open source development, firms obtain the direct benefit of software tailored to their own needs. The many firms that customize Apache represent consumers whose needs are largely not met by proprietary products.[34] In addition, open source meets the needs of firms that cannot develop their own software but that have the same needs as some of the customizing firms. And it also serves those consumers who cannot afford to license proprietary products. Open source thus provides a means to extend the market. Although it does not involve the exchange of goods for a positive price, it is an exchange of a software product for a (sometimes informal) promise to return possible enhancements to the community. That promise comes true frequently enough to sustain participation in open source development.

Of course, proprietary software companies can achieve some degree of customization by permitting third parties to make add-on products. But the third-party community for open source can be much more robust than that for proprietary products. For example, in contrast to Apache's 300 add-ons, the third-party listing for Microsoft's comparable web server product, IIS, contains the names of just 11 partner companies.[35]

There are two reasons for this difference. First, open source third-party development is just a counterpart to the open source process of code development; third-party add-ons are just those enhancements that the developer or Apache Group chose not to include in the standard Apache product release. But the developers of these add-ons have the advantage of full access to the source code, documentation, associated tools, and the advice (through email newsgroups) of the development community. This makes third-party development highly dynamic. Microsoft tries to encourage third-party development, and it recently announced a "shared source" initiative that permits select third-party developers to see, but not to modify, Microsoft source code. Nevertheless, it appears difficult for Microsoft or other proprietary developers to duplicate the kind of dynamic community supporting some open source products.

Second, proprietary software companies deliberately limit the role of third-party developers, choosing to develop some erstwhile add-ons themselves and preventing some from being developed at all. Third-party developers depend on application program interfaces (APIs) to integrate add-on products. Proprietary developers only make limited APIs available, and these change over time. For example, companies such as Netscape and RealNetworks experienced difficulty with their Microsoft add-ons as Microsoft changed APIs. Indeed, opening the APIs to third-party companies has been an issue in the Microsoft antitrust suit.

On the other hand, open source development is sometimes limited for another reason. The success of open source projects depends on a sufficient accumulation of code to make it worthwhile for developers to begin the customization-modification-improvement cycle. To some degree, open source projects face a chicken-and-egg problem. Until the project reaches a critical mass, it may be unattractive to many developers; developers may choose to wait for others to serve as pioneers. This is a version of what economists call the "free rider" problem.[36] Thus some open source projects fail to get off the ground where proprietary products can succeed.[37] However, once open source products do reach critical mass, they may very well prove superior to proprietary products at providing customer solutions.[38] And, fortunately, many of the alternative motives for programmers propel them forward.

In a way, standardized products and open source products are mirror images. Standardized products succeed by finding a common denominator of features that meet a portion of the needs of a large number of consumers. The market serves to aggregate demand, but the products do not satisfy consumers' specialized needs. On the other hand, open source aggregates *supply*: many different consumer-developers contribute modifications, enhancements, and fixes to meet a wide variety of different needs. However, to do so, open source projects need to begin with a common denominator of code that meets basic needs.

In summary, open source software meets a set of private economic needs that are not well served by proprietary software. The *Economist*'s false dichotomy posing "love" against "money " misses the reality. A profit-driven firm that is unable to purchase packaged software that meets its critical business needs may well find open source a rational and highly effective solution. For this reason, I believe that open source software will continue to thrive and become progressively more a part of the mainstream.

Open Source Software and Government Subsidy

Open source software allows consumers to meet needs that are not met by proprietary software. In a narrow technical sense, then, the widespread use of open source suggests opportunities created by market failure—that is, some socially beneficial transactions do not occur in traditionally organized markets. But this does not imply that government intervention is appropriate to correct these failures. In fact, open source software is itself a private means of remedying some of these market imperfections. In a broader sense, open source can be viewed as an extension of the market, a voluntary exchange between private parties. As such, direct government involvement is not needed absent evidence of other market failure. Open source has clearly flourished so far with little government support, and as the aforementioned SourceForge statistics suggest, open source is continuing to grow without much government support.[39]

One area in which government has a direct financial impact on both open source and proprietary software is in procurement. Various governments around the world appear to be tilting one way or the other. China recently rejected proprietary solutions in favor of open source products for a variety of projects.[40] In part, the Chinese seem motivated by a wish to cultivate a domestic software industry. Last year France announced support of open standards and recommended that government agencies use open source products, rationalizing the initiative as part of a plan to encourage the growth of small and medium-size software companies.[41] On the other hand, many existing procurement policies work against open source. For example, defense procurement in the United States requires security certification from the National Security Agency (NSA). Yet recent changes in the NSA certification process require the software vendor to pay the costs at commercial testing labs.[42] This effectively excludes much open source software. In addition, there appear to be some efforts to discourage or even to *ban* open source products from some defense procurement.[43]

Governments are clearly formulating different policies with different effects. The considerations are necessarily complex. However, I can suggest some simple guidelines. First, it makes no sense to have procurement policies that discourage consideration of open source products.[44] Second, most of the costs and benefits of any software purchase arise from the direct costs and benefits of the specific application. For this reason, products should largely be considered on their merits for the project at hand. Note, however, that when future modifications are important, open source may provide added flexibility, and thus future costs and benefits should be factored into the calculation. Also, whether the software is open source or not, systems should support free, open standards, so that future users need not be "locked in" to a particular product in order to access the data.[45]

Finally, it is true that there might be significant positive externalities associated with open source—that is, benefits that accrue to parties other than the decisionmakers. The Chinese and French governments appear to take this into account, viewing open source as part of a national "industrial policy" to promote competitiveness in the software industry.

But as earlier debates over industrial policy suggest, it is often very difficult to measure the potential benefits.[46] Indeed, it is hard to see what government procurement provides small software firms that they do not obtain from their own use of open source software. And while government support might help new open source projects get off the ground, many proposed projects are not socially beneficial, and government possesses no better knowledge than private parties about which proposed projects address unmet private needs.[47] Perhaps positive externalities can be demonstrated in certain cases. Nevertheless, the evidence to date does not warrant a blanket preference for one form of software provision over another.

Patent Thickets and the Future of Open Source Software

In another area, however, government policy may have a deeply chilling effect on open source development. Intellectual property rights regulate the exchange of software for both proprietary and open source products. Dramatic changes in patent regulation, largely initiated by the courts with little industry or legislative input, pose a significant threat to the future health of software and to open source software in particular.

Prior to the mid-1980s, trade secrecy law and licensing contracts protected techniques used in developing software. Copyright law protected against piracy. With these protections, the software industry was highly innovative, and in fact, most of today's leading software companies grew up in this environment

Figure 2-2. Software Patents Granted, 1975–99

Number of patents

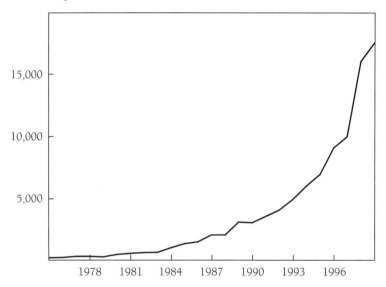

Source: Gregory Aharonian, PATNEWS, Internet Patent News Service (www.bustpatents. com [August 2002]).

lacking patent protection. The only apparent shortcoming of the system was its failure to provide employment for intellectual property attorneys.

That problem was fixed during the 1980s, when the courts engaged in a bold social experiment, extending patent protection to software. At the same time, they made other changes that resulted in a lower standard for nonobviousness and a greater presumption that any patent granted by the patent office was valid.[48]

The result was a dramatic patent "land grab" (see figure 2-2). The number of software patents soared to almost 20,000 per year, and a total of nearly 100,000 have accumulated to date. The largest share of these patents was obtained not by software companies, but by hardware companies building large portfolios—so-called patent thickets. Many leading software companies expressed the view that patents were undesirable, although many of these same companies have since been forced to acquire patent portfolios for defensive purposes.[49] Predictably, the number of patent lawsuits has also begun to soar.[50]

Open source developers simply cannot afford to play the strategic games in which firms with large portfolios of patents routinely engage. In a survey conducted by researchers at Carnegie Mellon University, 82 percent of the respondents said they patented product innovations to block competitors.[51] In other words, an important use of patents is to *prevent* innovation by competitors. Also, 59 percent said they obtained patents to prevent lawsuits, and 47 percent obtained them as aids to negotiations. That is, firms use patents, especially portfolios of patents, as bargaining chips. Many of these patents are never used commercially.[52] This behavior arises when technologies are complex, cumulative, and overlapping so that any single product may potentially infringe hundreds or thousands of patents. That's why semiconductor firms regularly engage in strategic cross-licensing of whole portfolios of patents.[53]

Software is very similar to semiconductors in that any single product contains hundreds or thousands of "inventions." Because large firms can acquire thousands of patents—a task made much easier thanks to the lowering of standards (see below)—they are beginning to play the same strategic games, and software cross-licensing agreements are the result.

Open source developers are well aware that they cannot easily play these games.[54] Individual developers do not have the resources to acquire sizeable patent portfolios. The process of negotiating and litigating portfolios is even more expensive. As Bill Gates wrote in a memo, "A future start-up with no patents of its own will be forced to pay whatever price the giants choose to impose. That price might be high: Established companies have an interest in excluding future competitors."[55]

Firms that use or promote open source have resources, and many also have large patent portfolios. Some, such as IBM, license their patents royalty-free to open source developers.[56] Other developers talk of responding to the emerging threat by building common defensive patent pools.[57] But to date, no significant patent

Figure 2-3. Example of a Trivial Patent

United States Patent   *5,851,117*
Alsheimer, et al.   **December 22, 1998**

Building block training systems and training methods

Abstract
A building block training system and method of training of cleaners of facilities to be used on the job which utilizes a plurality of pictorial displays showing a specific set of steps to accomplish a cleaning operation in an efficient safe manner, e.g., dusting or vacuuming of a facility as well as a plurality of pictorial displays as to what must not be missed and must be avoided in performing the cleaning operation.

Source: U.S. Patent and Trademark Office (www.uspto.gov/main/patents.htm [August 2002]).

pool or other organization has emerged that can protect open source products from such strategic competition, and the coordination and transaction costs of building such a solution seem quite high.

To date, only a few open source developers have been directly embroiled in patent infringement controversies.[58] Similarly, litigation activity and cross-licensing among proprietary software developers has only recently become a significant phenomenon. So far, patents have not had a major negative effect on software innovation in general or on open source development in particular. Nevertheless, open source developers are right to be deeply concerned about the possible emergence of patent thickets. Large firms competing with open source developers have little reason not to use patents as a strategic weapon. And a feasible defense strategy for open source developers seems problematic at best.

This problem largely arises because so many patents are granted for trivial inventions that are simply not significant advances over existing knowledge. Low standards allow firms to acquire large patent portfolios with expenditure of money but without commensurate innovation. For an example of a trivial invention, see the patent abstract shown in figure 2-3. This is a patent for a method of training janitors using illustrated manuals. Apparently, because the manuals have pictures, the patent examiners consider this a nonobvious "invention." They must not have read *Highlights Magazine for Children* in their youth. If they had, they would have found prior art in the "Goofus and Gallant" feature, which shows cartoons of the right and wrong way to do things. Another example is a recent patent for a method of swinging sideways on a backyard swing (No. 6,368,227).[59]

Now in fairness, these are unusually bad patents. But they illustrate the nature of the problem. First, the U.S. Patent and Trademark Office (USPTO) rarely corrects its mistakes. Even though both of these patents have been widely publicized, the patent office has only recently decided to take another look at one of them (the swing patent). Second, if the nonobviousness standard is low enough for backyard swings and illustrated textbooks, it is no obstacle at all for more technically obscure patent applications. Third, even though these patents might very well be found invalid if tested in court, litigation is very expensive. When large firms build portfolios of thousands of patents, it hardly matters whether many of them would survive a court challenge. The small developer cannot afford to find out.

The patent office, in fact, has little incentive to turn down patents since it runs on fees from successful applications. Not surprisingly, the USPTO declares that its quality goal is to "satisfy their customers"; their customers are not, however, society at large.[60] Not surprisingly, very few patents are rejected; if continuations (reapplications) are included, some 95 percent of applications are eventually approved, and few are ever subsequently reexamined.[61]

Some people claim that this problem could be solved if the USPTO had more money. Others suggest that patent quality will improve once the patent office develops better skills in new technology areas.[62] In fact, the USPTO just follows the standards set by the courts in this matter—for it is the courts that dramatically lowered standards. According to the 1952 statute, a patent should not be obvious to "a person having ordinary skill in the art." But since 1982, when a specialized court (the Court of Appeals for the Federal Circuit) was created to hear all patent appeals, this requirement has been dramatically eased.[63]

Court doctrine now pays great attention to "secondary issues," making it much harder to find a patent invalid because it is obvious. Prior to 1982, in court cases challenging the validity of patents, about 45 percent of the patents were found invalid for obviousness.[64] By the mid-1990s, only 5 percent were found invalid for obviousness. In effect, the federal circuit court has set a policy that permits large numbers of trivial patents in software and in many other fields as well. This policy threatens the future of open source.

Moreover, these government policies cannot be justified as necessary for the promotion of innovation in software. It is often argued that patents are necessary to promote innovation. In the words of the USPTO, "Through the issuance of patents, we encourage technological advancement by providing incentives to invent, invest in, and disclose new technology worldwide."[65] But in software, there is no evidence that patents have increased incentives to invest in research and development. The software industry was highly innovative before patents. Furthermore, Eric Maskin (Institute for Advanced Study at Princeton) and I found that the firms obtaining the large portfolios of software patents actually *decreased* their research and development spending relative to sales.[66] At best, software patents have thus far had a neutral effect on software innovation; at worst, they have had a significant negative impact on future innovation. And there is simply no evidence that patents are needed to promote innovation in software.

Indeed, large portfolios of trivial patents probably deter innovation even among proprietary developers. In the semiconductor industry, where large firms use patent thickets strategically, small firms end up paying a "patent tax" on innovation to the large firms. Not only must small firms pay royalties (IBM collects over $1 billion in royalties each year and Texas Instruments collected royalties over half a billion dollars per year by the mid-1990s), but the large portfolio holders gain access to the innovator's technology (so-called design freedom).[67] While the negative effect of these burdens has yet to be verified empirically, there seems little doubt that they reduce incentives for emerging firms to innovate. But although small proprietary firms may be taxed, open source developers potentially face extinction because they cannot even afford small patent portfolios and the costs of negotiating or litigating over them.

The prospects for open source and for software innovation generally would be much stronger if the radical policy changes imposed by the courts were reversed. Two sorts of changes would be helpful. First, Congress could restore the subject matter limitations on patents that largely prevented patents on both software and business methods before the creation of the Court of Appeals for the Federal Circuit. However, since the current crop of patents will last up to twenty years, this may not generate the desired benefits for some time.

A second change would reduce the strategic effectiveness of patent thickets by making their acquisition and maintenance more expensive. For example, rigorous standards for nonobviousness could be reimposed, and the doctrine of equivalents could be strictly limited. Also, a "polluter pays" principle could be applied to legal cases where infringement litigation is brought on patents that are found to be obvious (according to a stricter standard than at present).[68] Another way to clear patent thickets is to reduce their value. Penalties for infringement could be reduced, the litigation process could be simplified to reduce costs (for example, by eliminating the use of preliminary injunctions in infringement cases), and the term for software patents could be shortened.[69] Other considerations might level the playing field, allowing open source developers and individuals to obtain and maintain patents at little cost.[70]

These changes may be difficult, since many of them are likely to be opposed by the influential patent bar. However, the health and growth of one of the nation's most dynamic and technologically important industries is at stake.

Conclusion

Open source is an important organizational innovation in the development of software, one that improves the ability of private agents to meet private needs. It corrects imperfections in the market for proprietary software, and it does so without requiring government intervention through subsidies or procurement preferences. Procurement policies should permit government agencies to purchase open source software on the basis of its merits. In short, open source is a private solution that can and should be allowed to flourish without government intervention.

Unfortunately, the government is already heavily involved: relatively recent changes in the patent system threaten to disrupt open source software development. Over the last two decades, the courts have begun to supplant copyright protection, on which the viability of open source depends, with patent protection. The accumulation of large portfolios of software patents by a few large firms threatens to undermine this important social development. The actions of the courts need to be reversed to encourage the growth of open source development and the health of software innovation in general. Unchecked, software developers will lose much of their freedom to modify and enhance open source code, and with that, society will lose an important source of innovation.

3

Politics and Programming: Government Preferences for Promoting Open Source Software

David S. Evans

The Italians are doing it; so are the Brazilians, the Germans, and the French. Even Singapore is in on the act. And the list goes on: study commissions are cranking out paper—the European Commission alone has a stack of reports six feet high—and legislative proposals are coming out of the woodwork.

Global warming? Terrorism? No, governments around the world are thinking about making open source software—software in which the underlying code is accessible and thus subject to modification by users—the official pick.[1]

In the following I explain why governments should not give preferential treatment to one software production model over another in the contest between open source and proprietary software (in which the source code remains secret). The software industry has performed extremely well with little government interference. There is no significant market failure—indeed, production and innovation are both robust—that cries out for a government fix. Open source software that is available free of charge has done well when it offers advantages over competing software made by for-profit companies. Thus, tilting the playing field toward open source is likely to result in its use when it is not the best alternative. And unnecessary government involvement could throw sand in the wheels of one of the most important engines of the new economy.

For-Profit Software

Software firms make money by investing in code that meets some anticipated customer need. But once written, even the most complex code costs almost nothing to reproduce. Thus, whatever the price, almost all of the revenue from licenses goes to the bottom line. If others were free to use that code without compensating the owner of the underlying intellectual property, there would be little or no financial incentive to produce the code in the first place.

Today, the software industry comprises thousands of profit-oriented enterprises that create software and usually license the code for a fee. They typically distribute the product in "binary" form—digital code that cannot be read by programmers—that makes it hard for other firms to reverse-engineer their software. In addition, they use patents, copyrights, trademarks, and other forms of intellectual property protection that make it illegal to copy the software in any form without paying for it or to use the knowledge embodied in the software without permission.

Software firms that make a hit product—anything from a computer game like Myst to a computer operating system like Windows 3.0—stand to make a tremendous return. Firms that make duds—Microsoft "Bob" springs to mind—lose their investment.[2]

Overall, the software industry appears to be very productive. Output has risen twentyfold in twelve years, after adjusting for improvements in quality.[3] Revenue (measured in constant 2000 dollars) increased from $35 billion in 1988 to $171 billion in 2000.[4] By the same token, the industry appears to be highly competitive: over the last four years alone, the quality-adjusted prices for packaged software have fallen 27 percent in real terms.[5]

The pace of innovation, measured by the amount of money spent on research and the intellectual property created by that investment, has also increased dramatically. In 1986 research and development expenditures by publicly traded software companies accounted for about 1 percent of total industrial research and development in the United States. By 2000 that number had increased to 10 percent.[6] In 1986 there were 829 patents granted for software produced by U.S. residents; in 2000 the number reached 7,398.[7]

Compared to other industries, software production is not concentrated. The top twenty software vendors of packaged (as contrasted with custom-designed) software generate 61 percent of global revenues. The Herfindahl-Hirschman index (HHI)—a measure of concentration widely used by competition authorities that ranges from a low of 0 to a high of 10,000—was less than 244 for the software industry.[8] That compares with an average of 334 for U.S. manufacturing industries in 1997.[9]

The leading firms in the industry change places frequently. Of the top ten companies in 1990, five did not make the list in 2000, either because they went out of business or were acquired by another company or their share of software revenues dropped over the decade.[10] Compare this to the turnover in the pharmaceuticals industry, where success also turns on the pace of innovation. Eight of the ten leading pharmaceutical companies in 1990 were still in the top ten in 2000.[11]

The nature of competition in the software industry is different than standard bricks-and-mortar industries. It is dynamic, what is sometimes called "Schumpeterian" competition.[12] Competition is often *for* the market—a matter of winner-take-most—with everyone vying to be the category winner. Innovation and the ability to capture the positive feedback from so-called network effects—the increase in the value of a network when more people use it—matter a lot. Shaving two cents off the price does not.

The software industry is not perfect though—no industry is. Firms can become dominant in a category as a result of traditional economies of scale, control of key patents and copyrights, or network effects. Thus while consumers can benefit from the associated efficiencies, the dominant firm may have monopoly power and may therefore charge more than a competitive firm. This is a classic dilemma. One cannot hope to get the benefits of scale economies, network effects, and intellectual property without incurring the cost of some monopoly power. Courts and legislatures have implicitly acknowledged the impossibility of having it both ways. The antitrust laws do not make it illegal to obtain a monopoly through superior foresight, efficiency, industry—or even luck. By the same token, the copyright and patent laws formally grant temporary monopolies to those who create intellectual property.

No discussion of competition in this industry can ignore Microsoft, a significant player in two software categories and a perennial favorite for antitrust scrutiny. Windows is the most popular operating system for the personal computer, while Office is the leading business productivity suite. However, Microsoft is not unique in being a way-out-front category leader. Adobe's Acrobat document formatting software and Intuit's Quicken personal financial software are clear leaders in their respective categories. And despite Microsoft's tremendous success, its share of global revenues from packaged software is a relatively modest 11 percent.[13]

One could argue about whether the software industry is as productive or innovative as it could be. However, the question here is whether one can realistically look to the government to make the software industry work better than it does now, and whether government promotion of open source is the way to do that.[14]

Open Source

"Open source" typically refers to software that is released as source code with essentially no restrictions on what people can do with the code. Source code consists of the instructions—in programming languages such as C or Java—that programmers write and that others who know the language can understand. Thus programmers can modify, use, and redistribute open source code.

Open source software is usually created by cooperatives of programmers working over the Internet—a new-economy version of an Amish barn raising.

Open source would not have made significant inroads in some software categories if it did not offer value to some users. Indeed, the entrepreneurs behind the open source movement deserve a lot of credit. Ten years ago, who would have thought it would be possible to design really good software through a cooperative of unpaid workers dispersed around the world? Yet today Linux is one of the most successful operating systems for servers that store and transfer data for computer networks. It is also being used on handheld devices and cell phones. And IBM has reportedly spent a billion dollars refining Linux so that it can be used across its hardware line.[15]

What Is Open Source? Open source means different things to different people, and those who see open source in ideological terms can get quite passionate about the conflation of one flavor with another. As a practical matter, there are two sorts of open source, which are distinguished by the form of their distribution licenses.

All open source software is distributed with the source code readily available to the user. That allows anyone who obtains the code to "get under the hood" and fix bugs or create extensions to the code. Individuals and companies are always free to use open source software for their own purposes in any way they choose. For example, my company could use open source software within the firm, with or without customizing the software for my firm's specific needs.

The road forks, however, when it comes to distributing open source software. Some open source software is distributed under the Berkeley Software Distribution (BSD) license or similar licenses. The BSD license allows recipients to do almost anything they want with the code. They can modify it and distribute the modified code under a BSD license. Or they can modify it and sell the program as for-profit software, without providing the source code for the modifications. All the license obliges them to do is to acknowledge the contribution of the source code they have received from others. The list of companies and websites that use BSD include Apple, WindRiver, Yahoo, Google, Sony Japan, and many others.[16] In fact, at one time about 70 percent of all Internet service providers used BSD-licensed software.[17]

The alternative license form, the General Public License (GPL), is more commonly used these days for open source software. Anyone who distributes software that is based on source code covered by the GPL must release any variations of that software under the GPL.[18] As the proponents of the GPL put it, "We encourage two-way cooperation by rejecting parasites: whoever wishes to copy parts of our software into his program must let us use parts of that program in our programs. Nobody is forced to join our club, but those who wish to participate must offer us the same cooperation they receive from us."[19]

BSD and GPL both can boast of widely used open source products. Apache, Sendmail, and BIND are popular software for servers that all are distributed under BSD-style licenses.[20] Apple's Mac OS X operating system is based in part on software distributed under a BSD license. The Linux operating system is perhaps the best-known software distributed under the GPL. A variety of software that runs with Linux is also distributed under the GPL, including KDE, a graphical user interface, and OpenOffice, a business productivity suite.

The use of the GPL or BSD license divides the open source community sharply. Several prominent proponents of open source have advocated the greater use of BSD-style licenses to encourage the development of for-profit software that can work with open source. For example, Ximian, a leading open source desktop company, recently announced that some of its work on the Mono Project would be released under the X11 software license, a BSD-style license, rather than under the GPL.[21] This switch was supported by Intel, Hewlett-Packard, and the Mono Project leadership. Miguel de Icaza, a prominent member of the open source community and co-founder of Ximian, noted, "The X11 license ensures that the Mono project will attract a growing pool of talented developers, while enabling their companies to control and protect their Mono-based products and services."[22]

A larger and more vocal part of the community, however, supports the GPL. They promote the GPL because it ensures that the software will remain open and because it can push for-profit software out of the marketplace—which is an acknowledged aim of the GPL. Today about 80 percent of open source projects under development are based on either the GPL or its little brother, the Lesser General Public License (LGPL, previously known as the Library General Public License).[23] For this reason, government policies that promote open source software primarily promote software released under the GPL or its relatives.

How Successful Has Open Source Been? Open source software represents only a sliver of the product of the software industry some seventeen years after the concerted efforts to promote open source began under Richard Stallman's vision, and eleven years after Linus Torvalds posted the first version of Linux on a website.[24] It is difficult to obtain hard data on the use of open source because, in contrast to vendors of proprietary software, distributors and users of open source software do not necessarily leave a paper trail. Open source has achieved success in several major areas of software, including operating systems, file servers, web servers, mail servers, and development tools.[25] But it is widely agreed that open source has not made inroads in most business—and household—software categories.

Open source has found acceptance where the software is generally used by information-technology specialists, as with BIND, or where the software does not require interaction with consumers, as is the case with Linux on cell phones. How quickly and into what categories open source's sliver of the market will expand is a subject of much disagreement. For example, Eric Raymond wrote that "it seems safe to predict that open source development effort will increasingly shift towards the last virgin territory—programs for non-techies."[26] By contrast, Brian Behlendorf of Apache fame is skeptical. "Open source tends to thrive where incremental change is rewarded," he explains, "and historically that has meant back-end systems more than front-ends."[27]

Nevertheless, open source software has some practical advantages. Access to software at no cost can help to overcome reluctance to adopt software that is not already widely used. Allowing users to see and modify the source code may speed the testing and debugging of new software. By the same token, using the lure of community values to enlist the services of skilled programmers may reduce the real cost of creating software.

But proprietary software has proven advantages as well. It gives firms profit incentives to invest in research, development, and design. It gives them incentives to figure out what customers who are untutored in the fine points of software really want. Moreover, ongoing profits give firms the incentive to stand by their software—to make the myriad, unglamorous modifications that are the mark of seasoned, polished software.

The market is now sorting out the relative advantages of the two approaches. Open source seems to work well at creating software "by techies for techies" and software that does not require much of a human interface. It does not seem to work well at creating software for the mass market.[28] Perhaps that will change.

Some say that open source software is more innovative than proprietary software. That claim has no rigorous basis. No one has conducted a serious analysis of whether the open source method has led to, or is likely to lead to, more innovation than the for-profit method. Most research on innovation has focused on measuring the value of inputs (such as research spending) or outputs (such as patents)—an approach that obviously would not work for open source. Nor can one reach a valid conclusion simply by identifying several open source products that seem innovative; the same can be easily done for for-profit software.[29]

Although the open source method for producing software is an important organizational innovation, much of the software that is being produced under this method today is not innovative in the sense that VisiCalc (the first spreadsheet) or WordStar (one of the first word processors) was. Indeed, most open source projects under way are meant to imitate (or clone) existing for-profit software. Linux was an attempt to clone Unix.[30] OpenOffice is meant to replicate many of the features of Microsoft Office.[31]

Innovative or not, open source has had no problem getting traction where it can demonstrate some advantages. Otherwise, we would not be seeing Linux gaining share rapidly in servers and edging into embedded devices. Indeed, there is nothing stopping open source software from chasing proprietary software off the planet if it proves to be better, cheaper, or both.

That said, the hype is ahead of the reality. Open source software is cheaper than proprietary software insofar as one does not have to pay for the license to use it. But software costs for business are usually measured on a "total cost of ownership" (TCO) basis, which includes training and support.

Just how TCO compares depends on the products and the circumstances. Open source companies such as Red Hat make most of their money by selling training and support.[32] Open source code may have some advantages for companies that want to make sure their software is secure. But the computer science profession is debating the merits of different methods for making software secure, and it is not clear yet that having open source code is the best means to that end.[33]

Case For and Against Government Preferences for Open Source

Governments ought to pick the best products for their own internal needs. If open source software offers lower cost and better performance, that is what they should pick. Many businesses that have little in common with the Greens in the Florentine government have done just that.[34] Linux can be an excellent server operating system for certain applications. There are many other examples of open source software that businesses have chosen to use for the same reasons—they happen to be better, cheaper, or both. The German Bundestag reportedly picked Linux for most of its servers and Windows for its desktops because a study it commissioned found that was the best solution.[35]

If all governments were doing was picking the best technology based on cost and performance, there would not be much for economists and legal scholars to fret about. But in fact, there is substantial pressure on governments to give open source an artificial boost. Some proposals, for example, call for all government agencies to use open source software. Others call for giving procurement preferences to companies that offer open source software. Still others would require publicly funded software developers to release their products as open source. Even the Bundestag procurement process makes one a bit suspicious—since when do legislators spend their time dictating hardware and software choices for their back offices?

When Is Government Intervention Desirable? Economists have a framework for weighing the desirability of government intervention in the economy. It is a framework that is general enough and flexible enough to answer the question of whether the government should be doing something about global warming, regulating the electric utility industry, granting protection to intellectual property, or requiring truth-in-lending disclosures. To get from here to there, we ask two questions.

First, is there a significant market failure? Economists start with the assumption that free markets generally maximize social welfare. But they recognize that sometimes markets do not work well. For example, when left to their own devices, businesses pollute "too much" in the sense that the cost of their emissions to society as a whole exceeds the cost of containing the emissions.

Just because there is a problem, though, does not mean there is a solution. And that prompts the second question: Is there a government cure that is better than the disease? Government intervention costs money and can have unintended consequences. Even Joseph Stiglitz, who recently won the Nobel Prize in part for having identified a slew of fascinating market failures, acknowledges, "Recent decades have provided numerous examples of government programs that have either not succeeded to the extent their sponsors had hoped, or failed altogether."[36]

And just a decade after the collapse of the great socialist experiments, anyone who claims that the government should be picking software technologies has a heavy burden to bear.

Is There a Market Failure? The software industry itself does not scream out for government intervention. It has worked extremely well, and the success of the American software industry is widely credited to the lack of government involvement.

Even if it were true, the claim that open source software is better than for-profit software does not provide a sensible basis for government intervention, either. If open source software is indeed superior, information-technology specialists in business *and* government will use open source software. They do not need legislation or legislators to make that decision for them.

The closest I have seen to the identification of a market failure is the claim that the government needs to help open source become an alternative to Microsoft Windows. This seems to be what Lawrence Lessig is saying below:

> What reason does the government have for supporting closed code, when open code is as powerful and the externalities from using open code would benefit others? If the PCs that the government owned ran something other than Windows, then the market for these alternative platforms would be wildly expanded. And if the market for alternatives were strong, then the benefits from building for these alternatives would be strong as well.[37]

Professor Lessig's argument begins with the premise that open source is as good or better than proprietary software and ends with the conclusion that the government should promote open source. If he were a technical expert advising the government how to run its information-technology departments, I would hope that the government would thank him for his input and make the prudent purchasing decision based on all the information available to it. However, he seems to be doing more than that here and in his other writings.[38] He suggests that the government should be proactive about using open source software in ways that one would never suggest for a profit-maximizing business—or perhaps even for his own employer, the Stanford Law School.

There may be a type of market failure hidden in the passage, though. Let me rephrase the argument in the language of economics:

—Microsoft has a monopoly on the desktop.

—Its monopoly is partly the result of network effects: people want to use the operating system with lots of applications, and software developers want to write applications for popular operating systems.

—Monopoly is bad, competition is good.

—If the government buys open source, it will help generate network effects for Linux.

—Software developers would have incentives to write more applications for Linux.

—Linux would get more traction on the desktop.

—There would be competition.

—Consumers would win.

This argument fails at several levels. First, Windows is extremely popular precisely because consumers and developers place a high value on network effects—the more people who use Windows, the more valuable it is to each user of Windows and to each producer of Windows applications. Shifting volume away from Windows reduces those network effects. Not only is the government worse off, consumers are worse off as well. For example, complementary software could become more expensive as software developers would have to develop applications for a smaller audience.

Consider an analogy. The manufacture of a product sometimes involves extensive scale economies; so having two firms make the product results in higher costs for each. Would it make sense for the government to shift its purchases from the single provider to create competition? Almost certainly not: by diverting those sales, it would likely raise the price it paid because it would be buying from a smaller, higher-cost producer. Moreover, other consumers would face higher prices as well to the extent that their provider loses scale economies.[39] The same argument is true for network effects—if they are really important, then having a single provider is most efficient.

Second, if Professor Lessig's argument works for software, it ought to apply to many products the government uses that are subject to network effects—everything from telecommunications systems to credit cards. Although some economists have suggested that market forces might lead industries with network effects to become dominated by inferior products, there is little evidence of such "path dependence." And even some who take the path dependence threat seriously are skeptical that the government could manage network industries better than do market forces.[40]

Third, even if it made sense for the government to promote an alternative to Windows, there is no good reason the government should be in the position of preferentially picking winners.[41] There is no justification for exclusively backing Linux in particular or open source in general over, say, the Macintosh operating system—or Unix.

Fourth, the government cannot do much to stimulate the development of new open source products in any event. It is a relatively small purchaser of software within the global market. More important, unlike most products, the fact that government "demands" does not mean it will get "supply." Of course, it will get as much as it wants of existing open source code. But to get anything new, it has to depend on programmers around the world volunteering their efforts. A for-profit software firm in Bombay would surely respond to this opportunity. There is no reason to believe many volunteer programmers would. The government therefore cannot "make a market" for open source software like it could do for some products. All it could do is generate some small network effects.

Should Government-Supported Software Be Released under the GPL? The U.S. government has long funded research and development of software. This may well be an example of a sound government intervention in the market: it is widely agreed that for-profit firms do not have sufficient incentives to produce research to the point where the benefits—public and private—equal the private costs.[42] However, the government's decision to release some of the results of its software research under the GPL is problematic.[43]

The GPL effectively prevents profit-making firms from using any of the code since all derivative products must also be distributed under the GPL license. In other fields of publicly funded research, the government sensibly tries to disseminate the results widely and to help the commercialization of derivative products.[44] That is the right policy because it makes a public good—the results of federally funded software efforts—available for everyone to use, however they see fit.

Consider an analogy. The government funds university research that leads to a patent on a chemical that is important for the development of a new class of drugs. However, pharmaceutical companies must make further investments in research and testing to create a useful drug. Under the GPL approach, the government would require the university to license its patent only to parties who agree to license to anyone (for free) the subsequent patents related to the drug. That would prevent the pharmaceutical companies from realizing profits from investments that lead to further patents, thereby squelching their efforts to develop a commercial product.

The same is true for GPL software. Commercial enterprises would not make investments that required their intellectual property to be distributed under the GPL because, in effect, it requires them to make that intellectual property available to their competitors at no charge.[45] Consumers thus lose along with for-profit producers.

Software Patents. Some advocates of open source software have argued that software patents impede the development of open source software. They argue that the government should not issue patents for software.[46] This is an important policy issue that transcends the narrower question of whether the government should favor one form of software license over others.

Outlining the cost-benefit calculus for a patent system is easy. Patent protection is beneficial because it provides incentives for firms to invest in innovation. Without this protection, some valuable intellectual property would not come into being. But patent protection is costly because it gives market power to holders of intellectual property and leads to significant litigation and transaction costs.

On the other hand, determining where to strike the balance in specific cases is hard. It may well be that the standards for granting software patents should be tougher, so that obvious methods of solving programming problems cannot receive protection. It may also be that the lives of software patents should be shorter than for other products, since product cycles are shorter in software than in other industries. That said, I do not believe a solid case has been made for banning software patents altogether.

Conclusion

This discussion makes five main points. First, the open source method for producing software was a remarkable organizational innovation. It has shown that a cooperative of volunteers working over the Internet can create valuable software.

Second, there is no doubt that the open source method can sometimes produce software that performs as well as or better than software made by for-profit firms. Apache and Linux are quite popular in certain settings. However, these successes no more prove the superiority of open source software than the many for-profit successes prove the superiority of for-profit software.

Third, open source software is flourishing in categories where it offers better products at lower total cost of ownership. Linux has come from nowhere to account for a substantial number of server installations in a few years. It has outpaced Novell and is giving Sun a run for its money.

Fourth, no one has shown that there is a market failure in the software industry for which the imposition of open source offers a plausible solution. Governments should not be in the business of forcing open source software on the public anymore than they should be in the business of forcing the use of proprietary software. And they should not deny commercial companies the benefit of government software research and development by releasing this software under the GPL.

Finally, I am for government neutrality when it comes to picking software. It is perhaps human nature for government representatives—and economists—to believe that they can improve upon the operation of markets with unusual characteristics. Humility is in order. History shows that governments have no particular skill in choosing industries to support as part of industrial policy or technology-forcing initiatives. I see no reason to believe that governments would be any better at second-guessing consumers in the software industry.

4

Open Source Baselines: Compared to What?

Lawrence Lessig

Software is the set of instructions that makes a computer run. Programmers or coders write these instructions. The instructions then get translated into a form that computers can understand. The product of the initial authoring is called source code; the product of the translation is called object code. Humans write source code; machines run object code. Well-trained humans can read and understand source code; superhumans and computers read and process object code.

When software is distributed, the distributor makes a choice about whether the distribution will include both the source and object code. "Proprietary software" refers to distributions of software that include just the object, or binary, code. "Open source and free software" refers to distributions of software that include both the object and source code. With proprietary software, the consumer receives a program that he or she can run. With open source or free software, the consumer receives a program that he can run, modify, and—depending upon the license under which the program is received—redistribute. Proprietary software is like Kentucky Fried Chicken. Open source and free software is like Kentucky Fried Chicken sold with the "original secret recipe" printed in bold on the box.

And thus here lies the puzzle: by distributing the source code with the object code, open source and free software developers give their competitors free access to any value that they might have added to the software they are distributing. A developer thus cannot capture that value for him- or herself, but rather gives at least a part of it away. How then can developers have sufficient incentive to innovate? What motivates them to develop in this way? How can developers sustain the costs of development if they must hand to their competitors all the value they have created?

My aim here is to disentangle this puzzle. Open source and free software have played an important part in the growth of the Internet. The puzzle about their existence comes from a mistaken baseline of comparison. Properly understood, these movements are completely consistent with a tradition of innovation and development outside the context of software. They may seem unique within the software industry, but they are not unique against the background of development or innovation generally.

Using this appropriate baseline for comparison, the following discussion develops an account of the social value of open source and free software. This account, in turn, supports an argument in favor of the government adopting and supporting open source and free software projects.

Open Source and Free Software Defined

To the extent that there is sustained opposition to open source and free software, that opposition is targeted and quite narrow. Microsoft has been the most vocal opponent of a particular flavor of open source and free software development, an opposition that is subtle and, properly understood, specific.[1] But understanding this opposition and its relatively narrow scope requires a bit of background about the nature of free and open source software. And understanding the countervailing benefits from free and open source software in turn requires a bit of background about the relationship between software and what economists call "public goods."

The Nature of Open Source and Free Software. Open source and free software give consumers and the public something more than proprietary software does: the ability to tinker and modify. Such software gives the public the benefit of the information contained within the code. Yet open source and free software don't provide these values by forfeiting public law protection. Open source and free software are not "in the public domain." Copyrights still attach to their creative content. Thus copyright law continues to control how this content can be used and distributed. Open source and free software producers use this control to impose conditions upon the use of their code. These conditions vary significantly depending upon whether the code is free or open source. But these conditions are not options. They are requirements imposed by the force of law.

Not all software-related content is protected in this way. There are important software related products that are within the public domain. The TCP/IP (Transmission Control Protocol/Internet Protocol), for example, which forms the basic protocols of the Internet, is in the public domain. Anyone is free to implement it without the permission of a copyright holder. This enabled many to build TCP/IP networks inexpensively and ensured that no one had the power to control how TCP/IP would develop.

But being in the public domain also means that TCP/IP could in principle be hijacked. A major producer of TCP/IP technology could extend the protocol in a way that benefits its own interests and weakens its competitors. It could do this because the nature of the public domain is that anyone is free to build as they wish. HTML (Hypertext Markup Language) is an example of a protocol that was in the public domain. Netscape and Microsoft each tried to extend the protocol in ways that benefited its own implementation.[2] This competition may or may not have been beneficial to the spread of the World Wide Web. But whether or not it was, hijacking was possible because the underlying protocol was not protected.

By staying outside the public domain, open source and free software at least have the potential to protect themselves against the hijacker. Using copyright law, they have the power to require certain conditions before their code is used in ways that implicate the exclusive rights protected by copyright law. Thus, like proprietary software, open source and free software depend upon copyright; like proprietary software, open source and free software make themselves available only under certain conditions. The important difference among these three forms of software is simply the difference in conditions.

Proprietary software is made available upon the payment of a price (which sometimes is zero). In exchange for a price, the user ordinarily licenses the object code. Object code, because it is compiled into a form that is effectively opaque to humans, does not transmit the information it contains; it is simply a machine that induces another machine to function in a particular way. But attached to that machine is a license supported by copyright law. That license sets the terms according to which one may use the licensed machine. In the ordinary proprietary model, you are not permitted to sell the code you have licensed, nor are you permitted to modify and redistribute it. Proprietary code gives you the right to use the machine you've licensed, just like a rental from Hertz gives you the right to use the car you've leased.

Open source and free software impose different conditions upon users. And while the variety of open source and free software licenses is broad, we can identify essentially two sorts: copylefted software and noncopylefted software.[3]

Copylefted software is software that is licensed under terms that require follow-on users to require others to adopt the same license terms for work derived from the copylefted code. The principle is "share and share alike." Noncopylefted open source software imposes no such condition on subsequent use. With copylefted software, the price of admission is that if you redistribute modified versions of the copylefted code, you must redistribute it under similar license terms; with noncopylefted software, no such price is demanded.

The most famous example of copylefted code is the GNU/
Linux operating system.[4] GNU/Linux is licensed under the GNU
General Public License (GPL). The GPL requires that anyone
who modifies and redistributes GPL-covered code do so under a
GPL license.[5] For example, if an enterprising coder modified
Linux to run seamlessly Windows and Macintosh programs, he
would be free to redistribute that modified GNU/Linux only if
he did so under a GPL license. And since a GPL license also
requires that the source code of a GPL work be made available
for free, this Linux innovator would likely face competition from
copycat competitors. If the coder had in fact produced an operating system that could run programs from other operating
systems directly, then many would likely take it and sell it in
competition with him. The GPL guarantees that "freedom."

It is for this reason that some argue that the copyleft requirement is too steep a price for developers to pay.[6] The freedom of a
single developer to build a cross-platform-compatible version of
Linux, for example, might well be defeated by the copyleft condition (assuming that the costs of such a project are extremely
high and that the developer would need to recover those costs
from the sale of copies of the resulting operating system). But
this condition is not necessarily any more expensive than the
conditions imposed by proprietary code. If our Linux developer
wanted to create a modified, cross-platform-compatible version
of Windows, he would be no more free to redistribute the resulting Microsoft code than he would be free to distribute the modified Linux code under the GPL. If he could get the permission
of Microsoft at all, no doubt he would have to pay a high price.
The difference then is not that one licensing system imposes
burdens while the other does not; the difference is in the nature
of the burdens.

Noncopylefted open source software does not impose this
condition on subsequent licensing. Not only is a user free to
build upon it, but it also does not require that such building be
released under similar licensing terms. The Apache web server
is an example of this kind of software. Apache is an open source

Figure 4-1. Categories of Software

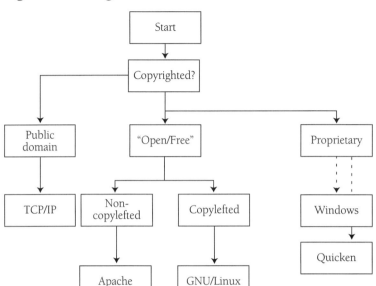

server, the most widely used web server in the world.[7] Anyone is free to download and modify the source code for the Apache server. And because Apache is not copylefted, anyone can take the source code and build it into his own software project. There is nothing in the Apache license that would prohibit a company from taking the Apache code, compiling it, and then selling the resulting server as a proprietary product (so long, at least, as it was not called "Apache"). These distinctions are mapped in figure 4-1.

No doubt, from a private perspective, the differences among these types of software are important. As you move from left to right on the chart, the ability of coders to capture the value of what they code increases. It doesn't follow, of course, that the income coders receive necessarily increases the further to the right they place their code, for the terms of the license could well affect the value of the software to others. One percent of a million is greater than 100 percent of a thousand. But as you move to the right, the legal right of coders to extract the full value from their code certainly does improve.

From the perspective of the public, however, another difference is significant. To understand this difference, however, requires a bit more explanation about the economics of software.

Software and Public Goods. As discussed above, software is a set of organized instructions for making a computer function. These instructions are written first in source code, which is then compiled into object code. The source code is understandable by the humans who write it; the object code is understandable by computers.[8] The product of these writings—a digital object stored on a hardware device—can then be copied at almost no cost. With the emergence of powerful networks, it can also be distributed at almost no cost.

This means that to some degree software has the attributes of "public goods."[9] A public good is not just any good that benefits the public. Food is a good that benefits the public; it is not a public good. As economists define the term, a public good is a resource that is both nonrivalrous and nonexcludable. It is nonrivalrous if your consumption of the resource does not reduce the amount available to me. It is nonexcludable if there is no feasible way to block you from consuming the resource once it is made available to me. National defense is the classic public good. Whatever level of spending the government provides for national defense, my consumption of national defense does not reduce the amount available to you. And if the nation is properly defended, I get that benefit whether or not I have contributed to its supply.[10]

Goods can be mixed—possessing both public and private attributes. Software is an example: it can be produced as a purely private good, but it can also be produced in a way that promotes certain public goods. These public goods might be divided between pure and "qualified" public goods. The information about how a program works—how it achieves its functionality—that is contained within its source code is a pure public good. If made available generally, then my consumption of that knowledge would leave as much for you as before. If made available generally, then it would be hard to exclude my knowledge of it to the extent that knowledge is known generally.

In contrast, the digital copy of a particular software product could be considered a qualified public good, meaning simply that it requires some resources in order to be obtained. My having a copy of your program doesn't interfere with your having a copy of your program. But it may take resources to produce that copy of your program. Likewise, an unprotected digital copy can be made available to all if it is made available to some, but it takes resources to move that content (the cost of electricity to run the network, for example). As modern digital technologies reduce these necessary resources to zero, this means in effect that software can be made available just as easily as a pure public good.[11]

The economics of public goods is, of course, well developed. If, following Elinor Ostrom, we distinguish between the *provision* of a public good and its *consumption*, then neoclassical economics tells us that social welfare is maximized if an *already existing* public good gets consumed at a price equal to its marginal cost of production.[12] That doesn't mean an economic system should require that its price be its marginal cost. If public goods could earn no more than their marginal cost of production, there would be an insufficient incentive to produce at least some public goods. If all the good that Microsoft produced by producing Windows XP could be immediately expropriated by every Microsoft wannabe at the marginal cost of producing a copy of Windows XP, then there'd be little incentive for Microsoft to build many of its products. If every song that Britney Spears recorded could be distributed to others for free, there'd be little incentive for Britney Spears to record as she does. With these public goods at least, solving the consumption problem (by making the goods available at zero marginal cost) creates a provision problem (by not creating enough return to support the incentive to create). Thus to maintain incentives to produce, such public goods require a way to defeat at least part of their own nature as public goods. In other words, what is needed is a way to make at least these public goods rivalrous or excludable, so that a price above the marginal cost can be collected.[13]

The law has long provided a device to achieve precisely this end—intellectual property. Intellectual property gives authors the right to control the distribution of copies of their work. That right balances the public goods character that writing makes manifest. The law levels the playing field for the publisher by giving authors the exclusive right to copies of their original work. Then de jure the work becomes rivalrous and excludable.

Software developers, however, have tools beyond intellectual property law that they can deploy to balance the public goods nature of software. Proprietary software providers, for example, can add excludability to their software by never releasing its source code: by compiling the source code and distributing just its object code, they can make the information within the product effectively excludable. Compilation makes the source code secret, and secrecy adds to the providers' ability to recover value.

Software providers can also make software effectively rivalrous. Copy protection technologies, for example, can make particular copies of software exclusive to particular owners. Properly deployed, these technologies can make it effectively impossible for you to use my software when I am using it. This again makes it easier for the producer to recover the value of his production by eliminating another public goods aspect of the digital product.

Thus two sets of tools—one public, the other private—are available to the software provider for balancing (or defeating) the public goods character of code. These tools in turn overlap. An author doesn't have to choose between copy protection technologies and copyright or between compiled code and law—he gets both.[14] And by combining both kinds, a producer will get more value and will, to some extent and in some contexts, increase the incentive to produce.

Yet at some point, the combination of this public and private protection may reduce, rather than increase, social welfare—at least if the protection is too strong. These protections raise the price of information above its marginal cost of production. This means less information is being distributed than is economically efficient. Economics resents a price above marginal cost. Any gap may be a necessary evil to induce production, but as with all necessary evils, it should be tolerated only so far as it is truly necessary. A gap may be justified by the need to solve the provision problem, but if the controls extend beyond the justification, they reduce social welfare. Some control is needed, but some control is far less than perfect control. And hence the problem of social policy is how best to balance a necessary evil against access to information at its marginal cost—that is, free.[15]

These familiar ideas are presented here to remind us of a point that is too often forgotten in the debate about open source and free software: the strong bias of public policy should be to spread public goods at their marginal cost. Compromises are no doubt necessary if private actors are to contribute voluntarily to the production of public goods; but public entities, such as governments, should not indulge in these compromises unless they are necessary. Between two systems for producing a public good, one that releases the information produced by that good freely and one that does not, all things being equal, public policy should favor free access. This is not because of some egalitarian bias or because of ideals about social equality but for purely neoclassical economic reasons: free access brings the cost of information down to its marginal cost, and neoclassical economics favors price at marginal costs. If the problems of incentives have already been solved for a particular good or class of goods—no doubt a large assumption, but for some important software goods a true one—then there is no further reason to exclude access to the public goods produced.[16] Or if the provision problem is sufficiently solved by other systems of incentive, then again there is no reason to exclude the public goods produced.

From a social perspective, this means that there is a difficult choice between these two forms of production. If social good is the sum of private and public goods, then we cannot pick between open and proprietary software in the abstract. On the one hand, open source and free software dominate proprietary software in spreading a public good. Yet on the other hand, if there is insufficient incentive to produce software under the open source and free software models, then the private good from software will also be underproduced.

When society faces a difficult social choice, that is usually a good reason to let both forms of production compete in the market. And thus no one sensible is calling for a requirement that all software be free or that free software be banned. Yet some do argue against open source and free software, sometimes motivated by a belief that its business model is a failure and sometimes motivated by a view that at least some forms of free software are dangerous to "software ecology."

The economics of open source and free software is just beginning to be understood. A growing body of literature increasingly demonstrates how individuals could have sufficient private incentive to solve the provision problem, even though they cannot capture the full value of what they produce.[17] The aim here is not to comment upon that work within economics proper but rather to clear the way for the lessons that economics is increasingly offering in the realm of public policy.

The following section connects the practice of open source and free software development to other more familiar instances of production. That link in turn will make open source development more familiar. It may well be that proprietary software maximizes the private return from software creation (though even that is questioned by some). But it does not follow that proprietary production is the only form of production that provides sufficient incentives for individuals and corporations to contribute to its supply. In this case, as in many others, an imperfect ability to capture the value of innovation does not necessarily destroy the incentive to innovate. And more important, increasing the ability to capture the value of innovation does not necessarily increase the incentive to innovate.[18]

Parallels

The system of production that produces open source and free software is not an exception within a free society. Properly understood, it stands on a continuum with production in most competitive fields. It is instead proprietary software that is outside the norm: its system of production is the exception, not the rule.

This positive claim does not entail negative implications for proprietary code. Its intent is rather to challenge a common assumption regarding open source or free software: that it is an exception within a free market, more akin to communism than capitalism. This view is mistaken.

Open source and free software are systems of production that mix private resources with those in a commons to produce goods or services of economic value. The production function thus includes both private and public goods, where the labor used to produce new code is a private good, and the information used to build upon the free software is public. The innovation and utility that this software produces benefits both the creator and the public. The producer captures some—but not all—of the value he or she produces.

Viewed in this way, it is easy to see that most production in a free market is structured in precisely the same way. Think about a coffee shop that opens across the street from Starbucks. It gets to draw upon lots of resources held in common—knowledge about how to attract customers, a taste for coffee, a taste for high-priced coffee—even though many of these resources might be directly attributable to Starbucks. Though Peet's Coffee claims to be older, it was certainly Starbucks that created the American norm for high-priced coffee.[19] That norm is certainly of value to Starbucks' competitors, but we don't therefore automatically assume that Starbucks has a claim to the value produced by this norm. There's no general principle within a free market that says that every quantum of value produced is the property of the entity that produced it. The value that Starbucks gets to reap from its innovation in coffee sales is just the amount it can make in the free market. As economists have long taught, the amount a business such as Starbucks makes in the market is a function of the demand for its product, the marginal cost of production, and competition. These may or may not equal the total value that Starbucks has contributed, but neoclassical economics was born with the insight that value received is not necessarily equivalent to the value produced.

Or consider a second example that is more familiar to the lawyer.[20] Think about the system of production called legal litigation services. Lawyers involved in litigation write texts to be submitted to courts; courts in response produce other texts that are published and made available to the greater society. The texts within this system are creative works (some more creative than others), but they are all fully available for others to draw upon and copy.[21] Opinions of judges can be used without the permission of the court; arguments from appellate briefs are fair game for others to use later on. All these resources are "free resources" in just the sense that free and open source software produces free resources. But none would conclude from this that lawyers are underpaid or that the legal system does not provide adequate incentives to lawyers. Instead the task of the lawyer is to mix new work with these existing resources to produce a result that benefits the client. The lawyer is paid for this mixing, even though the value of the mix is available for others to take.

The vast majority of coding in software projects has precisely the same character. As James Bessen has argued, most coding is customization—fitting existing resources to new uses.[22] Those who customize generate a product that is tailored to a particular user. Ordinary contract law gives the customizer adequate power to ensure a return to support that customization. Software coders in general are better off if there is a great deal of free software for them to draw upon. As with lawyers, there is no good that comes from forcing everyone to reinvent the wheel. And thus there is a public benefit if customizers contribute their work into a commons while also being paid for their particular customization.

These anecdotes point to a more general truth that, as William Baumol has quantified it, the vast majority of the value of innovation in a free market is not captured by the innovator. In other words, most of the value "spills over" into the market generally. And while sometimes reducing spillover will increase the efficiency of the market, as Baumol has argued, this assumption is not always correct. Sometimes the spillover is efficient.[23]

None of this is meant to argue that every software project should be open or free. Nor does it follow that lawyers should be unable to protect particular forms of their craft. My point is to show the ordinariness of systems of production where the producer does not fully capture the value he produces. That system is the norm in a free society. We call it a free market. It is not "theft" each time it is realized, and when it is realized, it can induce public benefit.

An example of this social benefit is seen today in the context of embedded systems.[24] As technologists find ways to build computers into every device around us, they need an operating system to run those computers. The free operating system of GNU/ Linux is the overwhelmingly dominant operating system deployed in these embedded systems. This is for obvious reasons. An embedded system producer wants to minimize costs, which include both the acquisition costs of software and the maintenance or debugging costs of that software. Because the GNU/ Linux operating system is free, the acquisition costs are low, and because many people have had an opportunity to debug the system, its reliability is extremely high. Thus the GNU/Linux operating system is an inexpensive and valuable resource for the embedded systems market. Without this inexpensive resource, the embedded market would not have experienced such a high degree of growth.

Others have suggested that there are more systematic benefits accruing to open source or free software projects.[25] As James

Bessen has argued, the costs of debugging complex projects such as software are so high that an open source project will often be able to bear those costs better than a proprietary project.[26] No doubt in many cases this claim is correct, as are other claims about the private benefit that open source or free software projects enjoy relative to proprietary projects. These are reasons why open source or free software projects could have a competitive advantage over proprietary projects.

Whether they have an advantage or not, however, my point is more modest. The phenomenon of open source coding is just one instance of a more general and familiar mode of production. Like most innovation within a free society, innovators cannot capture all the value they produce. The only relevant difference with open source and free software is that it chooses this "imperfection" whereas the others may not have any choice.[27]

Lessons

Finally, there is the question of government's attitude toward open source or free software. There has been a trend in many countries for the government to insist that its agencies use open source or free software. France, Germany, and China have recently announced such policies.[28] This, in turn, has pushed many in the United States to argue for the opposite. David Evans, for example, argues against governments favoring open source or free software in their purchasing decisions.[29] Microsoft, too, has argued against developing nations adopting GNU/Linux.[30]

Evans maintains that the government should make decisions about whether to adopt open source or free software in the same way as private actors should: the only question it should ask is what software maximizes efficiency.[31] I agree with his principle, but we must be careful about how it is applied to the particulars of the case, because the factors that determine efficiency for governments are fundamentally different from the factors that determine efficiency for private actors. Governments are not competitors in the sense that private actors are. They have a greater interest in externalizing benefits that other competitors might share.

Consider, for example, a government that is funding the development of an email system for its employees. That others could use the same code within the government if it were open source or free software would be one reason for the government to use such software to develop its system. Its code will produce a benefit for other governmental actors. All things being equal, that benefit should weigh in favor of the open source over proprietary code.

The same is true at the platform level. If the choice of a platform produces a positive externality for others within the government, this is a reason, all things considered, for the government to choose the software producing that externality. This is, for example, the argument used most commonly in favor of the government purchasing Windows as its base operating system. Uniformity throughout the government has its benefits. But it would also be beneficial to have uniformity at a platform level that was open. My point is simply that such benefits should be accounted for by the government as well.

Microsoft has questioned the propriety of government funding development of software covered by the GPL. In a series of public statements, the company has opposed the government's "support" for "free software," meaning software licensed under the GPL.[32] As explained earlier, open source software is not licensed under the GPL. Thus, Microsoft's argument says nothing about whether the government should adopt, for example, Apache web servers. The only target of Microsoft's attack is the GPL.

Microsoft's arguments are understandable, though how far they extend is hard to know. Microsoft argues that software licensed under the GPL has a "viral" tendency, as modifications to that software must themselves be licensed under the GPL. This means that some companies (in particular, some proprietary producers of software) are unable to use GPL code. This, in turn, could mean that projects operating under a GPL would become unavailable to companies such as Microsoft. GPL-based projects would therefore be developed and worked on only by GPL-friendly enterprises, which, Microsoft argues, could reduce the incentive to develop software.

At a formal level, one might well make the same charge against the government funding the development of proprietary software.[33] After all, if the government funds a proprietary software project, only the company owning or licensing the copyrights can participate in further development of that software. Other companies without access to the proper permissions are banned from developing this software. So just like Microsoft's claims about GPL software, these companies are precluded from participating in proprietary-software-based projects. By a parity of reasoning, it would therefore follow that the government should not fund proprietary projects either. By this line of reasoning, the only software projects the government should fund would be those that produce code in the public domain or under licenses similar to the dominant open source licenses, such as Apache.

As an argument about fairness, this ultimate conclusion might well have some force. But as an argument of efficiency, it doesn't quite work. If the test the government applies is which software benefits the government most at a given price, then it is not clear why the fact that it would exclude some private companies from developing that software should, on its own, matter. It could under certain assumptions matter, but in the abstract, it is hard to see just why the licensing choices of potential competitors should constrain the government in its choice of code.

Properly calibrated, then, government neutrality could well entail a preference for open or free software, depending on the program and the interests involved. More specifically, between two products, open source and proprietary, of comparable strength, there is a reason for the government to prefer an open source version. And between two products, free and proprietary, of comparable strength, there may even be a reason for the government to prefer the free software. This conclusion would not always follow, but it would follow for a wide range of code that today is not open source or free software.

There is a second type of neutrality that governments should also consider. This touches the question of software patents.[34]

There is not the space here to consider the full range of arguments surrounding the software patent debate. In my view, the debate shows conclusively that while there are clear costs to innovation imposed by software patents, there is no good evidence that they provide a sufficiently strong countervailing benefit.

The costs of patents, however, are significantly greater for open source and free software projects than they are for proprietary projects. The transaction costs of licensing are higher with open source and free software; the ability to license a patent is therefore decreased. This means that a system with software patents is biased against open source and free software. That bias might be justified if there were any strong indication that software patents do any good. But with the evidence pointing the other way, this is a clear example of partiality in which the government should not engage. Models of software development should be allowed to compete; the government should not allow bloated intellectual property regimes to tilt the field of competition against one of the most vibrant competitors.

Conclusion

There is a reason for public policy to prefer a world where software is open and free. That reason cannot trump all other considerations, and it alone does not support a general rule that would banish proprietary code. But the reason does motivate an inquiry into whether free and open source code can be adequately produced. Economists have just begun a formal inquiry into that question. That inquiry could be helped with a bit of perspective: by seeing the parallel between open source and free software production and other more familiar modes of production, we are more likely to accept the conclusion of economists that open code is often possible and often very valuable.

I have argued in favor of government neutrality regarding open and proprietary software—as long as the interests the government reckons are sufficiently broad. If they are, then the government will often arrive at the conclusion that open code is preferable to proprietary code. At the very least, such an approach would lead to the conclusion that the government should not allow software patents to tilt the competitive horizon against open code projects.

5

The Future of Software: Enabling the Marketplace to Decide

Bradford L. Smith

For well over two decades, people have debated the merits of developing and distributing software under what has become known as the open source model. As the name implies, the defining feature of this model is that it allows users to review and in many cases modify and redistribute the human-readable form of software known as source code. Supporters sometimes claim that the open source model produces software that is technically equal or even superior to programs developed under the commercial model pursued by most software firms.

At times, however, the open source debate goes beyond a comparison of technical merits. When comparing commercial to open source software, some advocates claim that the open source model generates a higher level of innovation than the commercial model, can deliver better economic benefits for local economies, and is even ethically superior to commercial software because it does a better job of promoting freedom.[1] According to this line of reasoning, open source is not merely a valid or even better model, it is the *right* model. For some, this conclusion also justifies the enactment of laws and regulations that favor open source software.

This chapter offers an alternative perspective on the open source debate, one grounded in three central claims. The first is that *both* open source and commercial software are integral parts of the broader software ecosystem. The open source and commercial models have coexisted within the software ecosystem for decades, and both have played important roles in its evolution. Moreover, recent actions by several leading software firms suggest that elements of these two models are beginning to overlap in important ways. Notably, this process is occurring solely in response to market forces and is not the result of law or regulation.

Second, the best catalyst for software innovation and industry growth is the marketplace. Only the marketplace, founded on a robust regime of property rights, can provide the combination of incentives and flexibility that will ensure not only that innovation occurs, but also that it proceeds in directions that satisfy actual market needs. Forecasting the twists and turns of this marketplace is notoriously difficult and beyond the predictive capability of any regulatory regime. While government intervention into the software marketplace may at times be necessary to correct specific instances of market failure, there is currently no such market failure that would justify regulatory preferences for open source software.

Third, governments can help promote software innovation and broader economic growth by supporting basic research. Such research generates the raw material that information technology (IT) industries utilize in creating new products, and many important software innovations are the product of private sector commercialization of publicly funded research. Governments can support this process by enacting policies that promote basic research by both the public and the private sectors. Governments should also ensure that the results of publicly funded research are not subject to licensing restrictions—such as those set out in the GNU General Public License (GPL) or similar "free" licenses—that would prevent industry from utilizing this research in commercial products.[2]

This chapter briefly compares the open source and commercial software models and describes certain aspects in which these two models are beginning to overlap. It then describes benefits of the commercial model that might be sacrificed by regulatory biases favoring open source software and examines steps governments can take to promote software innovation in a neutral, nonbiased manner. Finally, the discussion concludes with some thoughts on the future of the software industry.

Comparison of the Open Source and Commercial Models

Participants in the open source debate tend to use the terms "open source" and "commercial" (or "proprietary") to refer to three distinct categories of models: development models, licensing models, and business models. Analyzing each category separately helps illuminate key differences between the open source and commercial software models, as well as the ways in which software firms are beginning to adopt elements of both models within their broader strategies.

Development Models. Commercial software is typically created by a clearly defined group of developers who are paid for their work by a single firm. The firm, which normally owns the results of the developers' efforts, defines the scope and goals of the project, allocates work, and acts as a single point of accountability for the program vis-à-vis the outside world. In these respects, commercial software development is relatively structured.

The commercial development model is also customer focused in the following sense. Because commercial firms ordinarily generate revenue by selling or licensing their software, they have a financial incentive to identify—in advance and as precisely as possible—the needs of the market (which may include other developers, end users, or others) and to design their software to meet those needs as effectively as possible. Thus commercial firms have an economic incentive to link product development closely to market demand, and firms whose products most effectively and efficiently satisfy these market needs are the ones most likely to succeed.

Open source software, by contrast, is often developed by a relatively fluid group of volunteer programmers. The process of defining the project's goals and allocating work may be directed by a single person or group, or it may be determined by rough consensus. Similarly, ownership of the final product may be concentrated in one individual or dispersed among many hundreds or thousands of contributors. In these and other respects, open source development is less structured than typical commercial software development.

In contrast to the commercial model's customer focus, open source development may be characterized as developer focused. Because open source developers usually volunteer their time, they are relatively more likely to work on problems that they find personally challenging or rewarding and tend to be less concerned about whether these challenges respond to actual market demand. And since most open source projects do not generate significant revenue, these projects seldom have the resources to undertake market research or otherwise determine customer needs. Instead, open source projects often rely on releasing test or "beta" versions of software to gauge market reaction before arriving at a final version of the software.

Licensing Models. Although there are many differences between commercial and open source licenses (and between various types of open source licenses), the most salient distinctions relate to the terms governing
—access to source code,
—the right to modify the software, and
—the right to redistribute the software, whether in modified or unmodified form.

Commercial software developers typically generate revenue and fund future research and development (R&D) by exploiting the economic value of their software (specifically, the intellectual property [IP] embodied in the software) in the marketplace. While many commercial developers accomplish this by selling

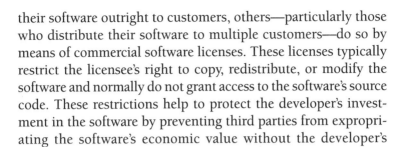

their software outright to customers, others—particularly those who distribute their software to multiple customers—do so by means of commercial software licenses. These licenses typically restrict the licensee's right to copy, redistribute, or modify the software and normally do not grant access to the software's source code. These restrictions help to protect the developer's investment in the software by preventing third parties from expropriating the software's economic value without the developer's authorization.

While the past decade has seen an explosion in the number and variety of open source licenses, most of these licenses fall into one of two categories. The first category includes what might be called "permissive" licenses. Permissive open source licenses allow licensees to copy, redistribute, and modify the software at no charge, whether in source code or object code, and do not seek to restrict these rights in any meaningful way. Thus licensees are free, if they wish, to modify and redistribute the software as part of a commercial product subject to standard commercial licensing terms. The Berkeley Software Distribution (BSD) license is a commonly used permissive open source license. Apache, a well-known web server software package, is distributed under a variant of the BSD license.[3]

A second type of open source license might be called a "restrictive" license.[4] Like permissive licenses, restrictive licenses permit licensees to copy, redistribute, and modify the software in either source code or object code. Unlike permissive licenses, however, restrictive open source licenses prohibit users from distributing both the code and any derivative of the code under terms that do not also permit subsequent licensees to copy, redistribute, or modify the program. Thus restrictive licenses prohibit licensees from modifying and distributing the code under commercial terms—or indeed under *any* terms that are not essentially identical to the original license. Because this restriction has the effect of replicating itself through all subsequent iterations of the software, these licenses are often referred to as "viral."[5] The General Public License is one of the most widely used restrictive open source licenses, but there are many others.

Business Models. Open source and commercial software are also generally identified with distinct business models. As noted above, commercial software firms typically generate revenue by exploiting the IP embodied in their software in the marketplace. In the case of prepackaged software, because most of the costs associated with the software are the up-front, fixed costs related to developing the product, vendors of packaged software typically pursue a mass-market strategy in which growth in unit sales brings down per-unit costs by spreading the developer's fixed costs over a larger number of units.

This business model has generated dramatic gains in the performance and functionality of commercial software products even as the price of these products has remained stable or even fallen.[6] The success of this business model has also fueled remarkable economic growth. For instance, from 1990 to 1998, the packaged software industry experienced average annual market growth of over 15 percent, making it one of the fastest growing segments of the U.S. economy.[7] The broader software industry employed over 800,000 workers in 1998, and the average annual wage in the core software industry in 1997 was $66,500, more than double the wage average for all private industry excluding the software industry.[8] The packaged software industry alone generated over $7.2 billion in federal and state corporate income taxes in 1997, a figure that is expected to rise to $25 billion by 2005.[9]

Open source software presents a more challenging business model. Although the lack of licensing fees has enabled some open source software programs to achieve significant market share in a relatively short period of time, the basic economics of the industry still require open source firms to generate sufficient revenue to recoup their costs and earn at least some profit. However, because open source licenses allow third parties to freely copy and distribute open source software, open source firms often find it difficult to capture the economic value of their software in the marketplace. For instance, Red Hat, one of the leading distributors of the Linux operating system, recently estimated that of the 15 million to 20 million copies of its Linux software package that had been distributed in the marketplace, only about 1.5 million had actually been purchased from the company.[10]

Red Hat's experience is not unique. Countless open source firms launched during the "dotcom" boom of the late 1990s have since been forced to downsize or even close their doors for good. Of those firms that remain, almost all are searching for new ways to generate revenue. These methods are often variations of a loss-leader business strategy, which involves distributing at a loss one thing of value (open source software) in the hopes that customers will purchase something else that will generate a profit (such as hardware, services, or even proprietary software).

Movement toward the Middle? Although the philosophical differences between the open source and commercial models are substantial, in practice, software developers of all types are beginning to pursue development, licensing, and business strategies that reflect elements of both models. Among commercial firms, two trends seem to be emerging. The first is to incorporate open source code into otherwise proprietary systems. Apple Computer's use of the FreeBSD UNIX kernel within the company's recently launched OS X operating system is one such example. Another is the decision by IBM to use elements of the Linux operating system as a platform for some of its commercial hardware and software offerings.

The second trend among commercial firms is to adopt attributes of the open source model into a broader commercial strategy. For instance, Microsoft's Shared Source initiative seeks to emulate the benefits of source code access associated with the open source model by giving licensees the right to review—and in some cases modify—the source code for several Microsoft platform products. Among other things, these Shared Source licenses enhance the transparency of the Windows platform and make it easier—at least for sophisticated customers—to debug applications and protect applications against viruses. The Shared Source initiative likewise fosters the growth of a strong community of software developers and IT professionals while promoting broad-based collaboration in the development of IT industry standards.[11] Shared Source licenses are proving particularly attractive to academic institutions, where access to source code is helping to foster a deeper understanding of Microsoft products among educators and future software developers.

On the other side of the spectrum, a growing number of firms traditionally identified with open source software are beginning to adopt aspects of the commercial model. For instance, several open source firms are developing and selling closed source software to complement their open source offerings. In addition, many open source companies have begun modifying standard open source programs in-house to meet the needs of specific customers or market segments. In essence, these companies are working to adopt what they perceive to be the best elements of the commercial software industry's development, licensing, and business models within a basic open source framework.

This phenomenon of software firms adopting elements of both the open source and commercial models is noteworthy in at least three respects. First, this process is taking place purely as a result of the market. Software firms are facing classic market pressures—from customers, from shareholders, even from industry partners—and are working to respond to these pressures within their broader business strategies by seeking to take advantage of what they perceive to be the best elements of both the commercial and the open source software models. Significantly, this process is taking place absent any form of government intervention.

Second, the ways in which software firms are responding to these market pressures vary tremendously. Whether this variety reflects a unique, short-term period of experimentation or represents a more fundamental shift in the software industry's development, licensing, and business models, remains unclear (at least at this stage). What is clear, however, is that consumers are benefiting from these industry efforts in the form of increased choices and greater competition. In short, this entire process bears all of the hallmarks of a well-functioning market.

Finally, it is worth noting that this process is making it increasingly difficult to classify any specific firm as pursuing *either* an open source *or* a commercial model. While this does not mean that the terms "open source" or "commercial" are no longer useful, it does suggest that merely applying these labels may reveal relatively little about how a particular firm actually develops and licenses its products or generates revenue. It also suggests that lawmakers should proceed carefully before enacting measures designed to influence the shape of the software industry based on a simplistic distinction between open source and commercial.

Strengths of the Commercial Software Model

Among the claims often made in support of the open source model are that it promotes innovation, promotes domestic IT industry growth, fosters interoperability, and provides a more cost-effective IT solution than commercial software. In reality, the commercial software model has a strong track record on each of these issues. The following sections explore these issues in more detail and examine their relevance to governmental policies affecting the software industry.

Innovation. Although quantifying innovation is notoriously difficult, two useful proxies for measuring innovation are investments in R&D and the impact of new products on users. By either measure, the commercial software industry is highly innovative. For instance, in 1998 the U.S. software and computer services industries invested an estimated $14.3 billion in R&D, which exceeded the level of R&D spending by the U.S. motor vehicle, pharmaceutical, and aerospace industries.[12] Furthermore, innovations in software have enabled businesses across the economy to become more productive. As a recent study by the Department of Commerce concluded, innovative new software programs have enabled firms "to create extraordinary efficiencies and improve decision making within their own operations and supply networks."[13]

The primary stimulus for innovation under the commercial software model is intellectual property protection. Software property rights give developers the certainty of knowing that, for a limited period of time, they and no one else will have the right to exploit the economic value of their software in the marketplace. By establishing this possibility of financial reward, intellectual property rights give software developers an economic incentive to develop innovative, useful products. IP protection also helps to resolve the free-rider problem that would arise if second-comers were free to copy and sell software programs without the original developer's consent.

Whether the open source model can match the commercial software industry's record of innovation is uncertain. The revenue challenges confronting open source firms make it unlikely that an open source industry could rival the level of R&D spending by the commercial software industry. And, while open source's unstructured development model arguably provides an avenue for the airing of unorthodox ideas that might not be available in some commercial contexts, translating even the best of these ideas into commercially viable products will often require resources that the open source model simply cannot provide.

This does not mean, of course, that the open source model is not an important contributor to software innovation. Indeed, many significant strides in software technology have their roots in universities or other publicly funded research labs, which are primarily based on the open source development model. In most cases, however, this research results in viable products only through the efforts of the private sector, whose incentive to commercialize this research depends on its ability to recoup R&D costs through IP protection. This complex process of interaction and collaboration between the public and private sectors—which itself constitutes an important part of the broader software ecosystem—should be nurtured, for it improves consumer welfare through useful new products while also fueling economic growth.

Governments have an important role to play in fostering such innovation. Because basic research constitutes an important resource for further IT industry innovation, governments can promote private sector innovation by expanding funding for university science departments and federal research labs, and by extending tax credits and similar incentives for privately funded research. At the same time, governments should support policies that facilitate the commercialization of the resulting research by industry.

For these reasons, governments should carefully consider the policy implications of using public funds to sponsor research that is licensed under the GPL or similarly restrictive licenses. As already discussed, the GPL forbids the commercial licensing of software that includes or is derived from GPL-covered code. Thus, if code developed in a government-funded lab is derived from or licensed under the GPL, the private sector would be foreclosed from using or building upon this code to develop commercial products. In short, use of the GPL in publicly funded research projects would drive an impenetrable wedge between the public and private sectors, thereby undermining the innovation and economic growth that has resulted from such public-private collaboration in the past.[14]

Local IT Industry Growth. Open source advocates sometimes portray the commercial software model as one that tends to favor entrenched players and leave few opportunities for newcomers. In fact, however, the commercial software industry includes thousands of profitable and innovative firms located all over the world. These firms have generated jobs, tax revenues, and economic growth in dozens of nations—including many in the developing world.

Over the past twenty-five years, the commercial software industry has evolved from a niche sector catering primarily to large enterprises into an exceptionally diverse industry serving customers across the economic spectrum. This process has created opportunities for existing IT firms and entrepreneurs to share expertise, create new products, and exploit new markets. Microsoft, for example, partners with more than 750,000 hardware manufacturers, software developers, service providers, and channel companies, including 350,000 firms located outside the United States.[15] Total IT revenues based on Microsoft products reached over $200 billion in 2001, meaning that every $1 earned by Microsoft generated $8 in additional revenue for firms offering complementary products and services.[16]

The beneficiaries of this IT industry diversification include developing nations. A recent International Data Corporation (IDC) study commissioned by Microsoft found that the IT industries in Argentina, Brazil, Chile, China, Colombia, Costa Rica, Czech Republic, India, Malaysia, Mexico, South Africa, and Venezuela experienced compound annual growth rates of anywhere from 6.8 percent to 43.7 percent between 1995 and 2001 and are projected to realize compound annual growth of between 6.3 percent and 26.8 percent through 2005. The number of IT industry jobs in these countries grew by at least 35 percent between 1995 and 2001, while eight of these countries—Chile, China, Costa Rica, India, Malaysia, Mexico, South Africa, and Venezuela—experienced IT industry job growth of 75 percent or more during this period.[17]

Commercial software firms have been important drivers of this broader IT industry growth.[18] The software industry is expected to grow 10 percent annually in 82 percent of the countries examined by IDC (which includes all of the developing countries listed above).[19] In a separate study commissioned by the Business Software Alliance, PricewaterhouseCoopers calculated that the packaged software industry alone generated an estimated $21 billion in annual tax revenues during 1996–97 for non–U.S. governments, a figure that was projected to reach $34 billion in 2001.[20]

India's IT industry illustrates the benefits that developing nations can realize from the commercial software model. Between 1994–95 and 2000–01, gross earnings from the Indian software industry grew from $835 million to $8.2 billion, while the value of software exports grew from $485 million to $6.2 billion.[21] India had over 16,000 IT firms in 2001 (double the number of firms just six years earlier), which employed over 561,000 workers.[22] Overall IT spending in India grew an average of 20.6 percent annually from 1995 to 2001 and is expected to increase to 26 percent annually from 2001 to 2005.[23]

Whether the open source model can provide similar economic opportunities for nations working to develop domestic IT industries remains to be seen. Given the significant revenue challenges currently facing open source firms, however, it seems at best premature to suggest that the open source model provides a more certain path to economic growth than the commercial model.

Interoperability. The commercial software model is also an important driver of interoperability. Commercial developers promote interoperability through industry-wide standardization efforts and through their support of market-based standards. Indeed, there are reasons to believe that the commercial software model may do a better job of promoting interoperability than the open source model.

Commercial software firms have historically been active contributors to broad-based IT standards bodies, and Microsoft's efforts in this area are no exception. Microsoft participates in every leading IT standards body, including the Internet Engineering Task Force (IETF), the World Wide Web Consortium (W3C), the European Computer Manufacturers Association (ECMA), the Web Services Interoperability Organization (WS-I), and many others. Microsoft also encourages its researchers to publish the results of their work and in this way to contribute to the knowledge "commons" from which broad-based IT standards are often born.[24] The commercial software model has also promoted interoperability through the creation of market-based standards and through the popularization of computing platforms like UNIX and Windows.

The result of these various efforts is that literally thousands of off-the-shelf hardware and software products on the market today can communicate and exchange data. Further evidence of these efforts can be seen in the IT systems of large enterprises, which often include a range of hardware, software, and platform products from several different vendors. Whereas sharing data between the disparate elements of these systems typically would have been difficult or impossible only seven or eight years ago, industry efforts since then to promote open standards—including support for the Internet as a common communications layer—have helped to create an environment today in which data can be shared among most elements of these IT systems with much greater ease.

The most significant recent example of the commercial software model's promotion of IT interoperability is embodied in a group of standards based on the Internet format XML, which stands for "eXtensible Markup Language." XML is an open standard maintained by the W3C that is available to all on a royalty-free basis.[25] Although the technologies that support XML are sophisticated, the XML vision is simple: use open, industry-wide standards to enable applications running on any platform and written in almost any programming language to interoperate with one another.

Microsoft, together with several other leading commercial software vendors, has contributed millions of dollars to help develop the basic XML architecture. Microsoft has also submitted key elements of its implementation of XML—known as the Microsoft .NET framework—to ECMA, Europe's leading IT standards body, for standardization. ECMA members recently adopted and published as open standards two Microsoft technologies—its Common Language Infrastructure and its C# programming language—which means that these technologies are now freely available for use by anyone. In addition, Microsoft has worked closely with the nonprofit MONO project to develop open source implementations of the basic .NET infrastructure.

The IT industry's recent history demonstrates that the commercial software industry thrives when IT interoperability flourishes. By working closely with IT standards bodies and other IT firms, commercial software vendors have helped drive significant improvements in IT interoperability in recent years and are likely to continue to do so for the foreseeable future.

Cost-effectiveness. Another claim often made in support of the open source model is that open source software is more cost-effective than commercial software. Because (the argument goes) users can freely load open source programs (depending on how they are licensed) on as many computers as they like without incurring additional license fees, they can channel the resources saved to other more productive uses. In fact, however, many factors besides software license fees contribute to the overall cost-effectiveness of an IT system—factors that can make systems based on open source software *less* cost-effective in the long run than those based on commercial software.

First, software licenses normally comprise a minor component of the purchase price of a complete IT system. Moreover, an IT system's purchase price usually forms only a small portion of its total cost of ownership (TCO), which is typically dominated by postpurchase costs, such as customizing the system to the user's specific needs, maintaining and servicing the system, and training costs. In fact, software acquisition costs are often less than 5 percent of the overall cost of an enterprise system. An accurate assessment of cost must also take into account a system's return on investment. For instance, if a system with a higher purchase price enables an organization's workers to be more productive than one with a lower purchase price, the higher-priced system may provide a quicker return on investment—and thus be more cost-effective—than the lower-priced alternative.

Although few independent analysts have examined rigorously the relative TCO of IT systems based on open source software as compared to those based on commercial software, there is fairly broad consensus that software license fees have relatively little impact on a system's TCO. As one open source commentator recently observed, "Every analyst has a proprietary total-cost-of-ownership model, and everyone's equation is slightly different. But they all show that the low cost of acquiring free software is not a significant benefit when amortized over the lifetime costs of the system."[26]

In addition, several analysts that have examined the issue have noted that because open source solutions tend to be more customized than their commercial counterparts, open source solutions will often require more sophisticated (and thus more expensive) support and maintenance. Moreover, IT services often prove quite difficult to scale in a cost-effective manner. For these reasons, IT systems using commercial software may, in many cases, prove more cost-effective to operate in the long run than similar systems based on open source software.[27] As analysts at the independent IT research firm META Group concluded, "Linux is typically not a low-cost alternative [as compared to Microsoft Windows] when viewed from a total-cost-of-ownership perspective, because it costs more for organizations to support it."[28]

More fundamentally, it remains open to question whether the open source model will be able to replicate several key efficiencies that are now commonplace in the commercial software industry. As already discussed, the emergence of standardized platforms and interfaces has made it possible for many commercial vendors to pursue mass-market business strategies and thereby to realize significant economies of scale. The absence of constraints on modifying software under the open source model, by contrast, suggests that open source vendors may find it significantly more difficult to achieve similar economies of scale.

The Future of Software

The open source and commercial software models have been critical elements of the software ecosystem for decades, and both are likely to continue to play important roles in the years ahead. Recent events suggest that firms across the industry are now working to incorporate what they perceive to be the best elements of both models in their broader strategies. Although it is difficult to predict the final result of this process, it is much easier to predict that the principal beneficiaries of this process will be consumers in the form of more choices and lower prices.

This prediction, however, rests on two assumptions. The first is that the marketplace will determine the path along which the software industry evolves. Only the marketplace—comprised of thousands of developers and firms reacting to millions of customer decisions every day—offers both the flexibility and incentives necessary to ensure that software innovation proceeds in a direction that satisfies actual consumer needs. And the marketplace can function effectively only if it is based upon a clear regime of property rights and if government intervention is limited to addressing specific instances of market failure.

The second assumption is that governments will continue to invest in basic IT research. Publicly funded research has played a critical factor in the success of the U.S. IT industry by helping to create a bedrock of technical knowledge that industry can then develop into commercially useful products. As long as such research is made available under terms that do not limit its utilization in commercial products, this research will be an extremely important resource for continued innovation in the software industry. This combination of a robust, open marketplace and public support for IT research will provide the groundwork for a diverse, competitive and innovative software ecosystem.

Notes

Chapter 1
Government Policy toward Open Source Software:
An Overview

1. Certainly not all users could modify the code and still get the program to work. But the code is available in a form that allows anyone who knows (or is willing to learn) the programming language to modify it. For a more precise definition, see the discussion in chapter 4.

Software programs are written in languages, such as C++ or Java, that people trained in the language can easily understand. Programming languages are usually similar to spoken language, using phrases such as "if . . . then," "else," and "do." The code written in a programming language is referred to as source code. Source code is then translated (or compiled) into a language that the computer can understand. This code, referred to as binary code (or sometimes machine code or object code), is a series of ones and zeros and, as such, is extremely difficult for even accomplished programmers to decipher. See discussion in chapters 3 and 4.

2. The Free Software Foundation (FSF), headed by Richard Stallman, distinguishes between free and open source software. As Stallman writes, "The obvious meaning for 'open source software' is 'You can look at the source code.' This is a much weaker criterion than 'free software.'" See "Why 'Free Software' Is Better than 'Open Source'" (www.fsf.org/philosophy/free-software-for-freedom.html [May 10, 2001]). In contrast, "'Free software,'" Stallman writes, "is a matter of liberty . . . you should be free to redistribute copies, either with or without modifications, either gratis or charging a fee for distribution, to anyone anywhere. Being free to do these things means (among other things) that you do not have to ask or pay for permission." See "The Free Software Definition" (www.fsf.org/philosophy/free-sw.html [June 27, 2002]).

3. See the Linux home page for additional information (www.linux.org).

4. See, respectively, "Sendmail Company Overview" (www.sendmail.com/company/overview [May 11, 2001]), the Apache Software Foundation (www.apache.org [June 27, 2002]), and Sun Microsystems product web page for StarOffice (www.sun.com/software/star/staroffice/6.0/index.html [June 27, 2002]).

5. International Data Corporation (IDC), one of the leading providers of industry analysis and market data for information technology products and services, did not include Linux in its market analysis until 2001. "If there is one big story from a shipment perspective, it would be that new license sales of Linux SOEs [server operating environments] mushroomed during 1999. In fact, Linux surpassed NetWare as the number 2 SOE in shipments, an event IDC previously had projected to happen much further out in the forecast period." See Vernon Turner and others, "Worldwide Server Market Forecast and Analysis, 2001–2005," report 25031, June 2001, p. 21 (www.idcresearch.com [July 29, 2002]).

6. On incentives governing the production of open source software, see, for example, Josh Lerner and Jean Tirole, "The Simple Economics of Open Source," *Journal of Industrial Economics*, vol. 50, no. 2 (2002), pp. 197–234. For a general introduction to the economics literature on open source, see Aaron Schiff, "The Economics of Open Source Software: A Survey of the Early Literature," *Review of Network Economics*, vol. 1, no. 1 (2002), pp. 66–74.

7. See the Logitas website (www.logitas.com/english/ownership.php3 [July 9, 2002]); see also Dennis S. Deutsch, "Trade Secret Protection for Software," *Computer Forensics Online* (www.shk-dplc.com/cfo/issue%201/secret.html [June 9, 2002]).

8. "The goal of the GPL is to grant everyone the freedom to copy, redistribute, understand, and modify a program. If you could incorporate GPL-covered software into a non-free system, it would have the effect of making the GPL-covered software non-free too. . . . The GPL says that any extended version of the program must be released under the GPL if it is released at all. This is for two reasons: to make sure that users who get the software get the freedom they should have, and to encourage people to give back improvements that they make." Free Software Foundation, "FAQs" (www.fsf.org/licenses/gpl-faq.html#whyusegpl [June 28, 2002]).

9. Still more governments have proposed or adopted nonbinding legislation that suggests using open source software instead of proprietary products. For example, several municipal governments in Italy (including Florence) passed laws in the spring of 2002 suggesting that all government offices gradually shift to Linux. See www.prosa.it/philosophy/successi/index.shtml (in Italian [July 12, 2002]).

10. For a more complete definition of market failure, see Dennis W. Carlton and Jeffrey M. Perloff, *Modern Industrial Organization*, 2d ed. (Boston: Addison-Wesley, 1994), p. 115.

11. Some might argue that a substantial margin is too high a threshold for intervention, but if a particular policy intervention is likely to yield only small

net benefits, I believe it is probably not worth doing—in part, because the government or policymaker can probably do other things that have a higher payoff.

12. See the section "Software and Public Goods" in chapter 4.

13. Certainly private companies, especially larger ones with multiple offices, are concerned with standardization. Sharing documents and working jointly is much more difficult in an environment without standard software. Private firms could equally value "openness." For example, a firm might find that customizing open source software, say Linux, provides a certain degree of standardization but also allows internal departments to shape the software to their own needs.

14. If government-funded software is licensed under the GPL, all other programs that incorporate or extend that software must be licensed under GPL. As a result, the government-funded project could not form the basis for a commercial product—it must remain GPL instead. If the government funded proprietary research, it would remain secret (with source code not shared) and therefore would not be available for others to use. However, the owner of the code would have profit incentives to make the code valuable to users, which might lead to licensing of the code to others. If the government-funded software is licensed under a less restrictive open source license, like BSD, then it can be incorporated into commercial products as well as used in other open source projects. A policy requiring BSD-style licensing for government-funded software research could therefore support both the proprietary *and* the commercial software sectors of the market.

Chapter 2
What Good Is Free Software?

1. See the Netcraft Web Server Survey, "Market Share for Top Servers across All Domains, August 1995–July 2002" (www.netcraft.com/survey/ [August 2002]). "Open source" software refers to software in which the source code that programmers use to create the software is freely accessible. This means that the product is freely available to all users and that any programmer can modify, debug, and enhance the product.

2. Audris Mockus, Roy T. Fielding, and James Herbsleb, "A Case Study of Open Source Software Development: The Apache Server," paper prepared for the 22d International Conference on Software Engineering, Limerick, Ireland (http://opensource.mit.edu/papers/mockusapache.pdf [August 2002]).

3. This model is developed more formally in James Bessen, "Open Source Software: Free Provision of Complex Public Goods," ROI Working Paper, July 2002 (www.researchoninnovation.org/opensrc/pdf [August 2002]). This formal analysis is quite similar to the explanation provided by Nikolaus Franke and Eric von Hippel, "Satisfying Heterogeneous User Needs via Innovation Toolkits: The Case of Apache Security Software," Working Paper 4341-02, Sloan School

of Management, Massachusetts Institute of Technology, January 2002 (http://opensource.mit.edu/papers/frankevonhippel.pdf [August 2002]).

4. Josh Lerner and Jean Tirole, "The Simple Economics of Open Source," Working Paper 7600 (Cambridge, Mass.: National Bureau of Economic Research, March 2000); Justin Pappas Johnson, "Economics of Open Source Software," unpublished working paper, May 17, 2001; Jennifer Kuan, "Open Source Software as Consumer Integration into Production," unpublished working paper, October 26, 2000. In addition, researchers from a variety of other disciplines have studied open source software. A collection of working papers, including these, is available at http://opensource.mit.edu/papers [August 2002].

5. Robert Parker and Bruce Grimm, *Recognition of Business and Government Expenditures for Software as Investment: Methodology and Quantitative Impacts, 1959–98*, report presented at the meeting of the Bureau of Economic Analysis, May 5, 2000 (www.bea.doc.gov/bea/papers/software.pdf [August 2002]).

6. For a general history, see Glyn Moody, *Rebel Code: The Inside Story of Linux and the Open Source Revolution* (Cambridge, Mass.: Perseus Publishing, 2001).

7. Richard Stallman, "The Free Software Definition" (www.fsf.org/philosophy/free-sw.html [August 2002]).

8. For a review, see Erik Brynjolfsson and Lorin M. Hitt, "Beyond Computation: Information Technology, Organizational Transformation and Business Performance," *Journal of Economic Perspectives*, vol. 14, no. 4 (2000), pp. 23–48.

9. See, for example, David S. Evans, "Is Free Software the Wave of the Future?" *Milken Institute Review*, 4th quarter (2001), p. 41. His current views, however, appear to have changed.

10. "Out in the Open," *Economist*, April 14, 2001, special section, p. 8.

11. Netcraft Web Server Survey, "Market Share." See also David A. Wheeler, "Why Open Source Software/Free Software (OSS/FS)? Look at the Numbers!" 2002 (www.dwheeler.com/oss_fs_why.html [August 2002]).

12. Barton P. Miller and others, "Fuzz Revisited: A Re-examination of the Reliability of UNIX Utilities and Services," working paper, University of Wisconsin, 1995 (ftp://grilled.cs.wisc.edu/technical_papers/fuzz-revisited.pdf); Kuan, "Open Source."

13. "The Revenge of the Hackers," *Economist*, July 9, 1998, p. 63.

14. Karim R. Lakhani, Bob Wolf, and Jeff Bates, "The Boston Consulting Group Hacker Survey," January 31, 2002 (www.osdn.com/bcg/bcg/bcghacker survey.html [August 2002]).

15. Evans, "Free Software," p. 41.

16. See www.kde.org and www.gnome.org.

17. See Rex Baldazo, "CNET Review: Mozilla 1.0 Release Candidate 2," May 14, 2002 (www.cnet.com/software/0-3227883-8-9895059-1.html?tag=st.sw.3227883.bhed.3227883-8-9895059-1 [August 2002]), and Andrew Leonard, "Mozilla's Revenge," *Salon*, March 12, 2002 (www.salon.com/tech/col/leon/2002/03/12/mozilla/ [August 2002]).

18. On the other hand, there is a model that shows that open source has a

comparative advantage over the proprietary provision of complex applications. See Bessen, "Open Source Software." This model suggests that the technically sophisticated nature of much open source software arises from an economic decision, not a fundamental limitation in the open source development process.

19. www.sourceforge.net.

20. Wylie Wong, "Application Server Giants Regroup," *CNET*, December 3, 2001 (www.news.com.com/2100-1001-276459.html?legacy=cnet&tag= st.ne.ni.gartnercomm.ni [August 2002]).

21. Ibid.

22. See also Lerner and Tirole, "Simple Economics of Open Source."

23. For example, David Coursey, "And Today, Microsoft Is Still Driving Me Nuts (Part Two)," May 7, 2001 (www.zdnet.com/anchordesk/stories/story/0,10738,2715734,00.html [August 2002]).

24. These issues are discussed in Michael A. Cusumano and Richard W. Selby, *Microsoft Secrets: How The World's Most Powerful Software Company Creates Technology, Shapes Markets and Manages People* (Simon and Schuster, 1995).

25. See Bessen, "Open Source Software"; and Cusumano and Selby, *Microsoft Secrets*, especially p. 310.

26. Generally, asymmetric information describes a situation where one party (or group of parties) has private information that another party (or parties) does not have.

27. There is an additional factor limiting provision under custom proprietary development. In many cases custom development uses an application program interface (API) provided by a standardized software firm. However, monopoly pricing of this API implies a deadweight loss—some consumers will be priced out of the market. See Bessen, "Open Source Software."

28. Franke and von Hippel, "Satisfying Heterogeneous User Needs," provide some evidence for this.

29. Ibid. Security features represent only a fraction of Apache's total feature set, so presumably the total extent of customization is even greater.

30. "Apache Module Registry" (http://modules.apache.org/ [May 25, 2002, with duplicates and bad records eliminated]).

31. "Apache Module Report" (https://secure1.securityspace.com/s_survey/data/man.200204/apachemods.html [May 25, 2002]).

32. Mockus, Fielding, and Herbsleb, "A Case Study."

33. Ibid., table 1.

34. Note that very little of the customization effort can be attributed to firms attempting to economize by using a free product and then correcting deficiencies through customization. The second most popular web server, Microsoft's IIS, is free for users of the Windows operating system. Apache runs on Linux (free), proprietary Unix, and also on Windows. If one assumes that these operating systems are equivalent for running web servers, then Apache offers no direct cost saving relative to IIS. Even if Linux were inferior to Windows but could be fixed through customization of Apache, the cost difference would be

minor—the price of Windows is $300 or less per license. Thus few firms would plausibly customize Apache to compensate for major deficiencies in Linux.

35. "IIS-Enabled Products from Industry Partners" (www.microsoft.com/windows2000/partners/iis.asp [May 25, 2002]).

36. See Johnson, "Economics of Open Source."

37. Of course, some proprietary products experience "network externalities" and may also face similar chicken-and-egg problems.

38. See endnotes 12 through 14.

39. www.sourceforge.net.

40. "Linux Takes on MS in China," BBC News, January 8, 2002 (http://news.bbc.co.uk/hi/english/sci/tech/newsid_1749000/1749441.stm [August 2002]).

41. Rick Perera, "Open-source Fans Welcome French Government," ITWorld.com, November 26, 2001 (www.itworld.com/Man/2685/IDG011126frenchopensource/ [August 2002]).

42. See http://niap.nist.gov/cc-scheme/historical-perspective.html [August 2002]).

43. Jonathan Krim, "Open-Source Fight Flares at Pentagon: Microsoft Lobbies Hard against Free Software," Washington Post, May 23, 2002, p. E1.

44. Ken Brown argues that open source poses a security risk; see Opening the Open Source Debate (Washington: Alexis de Tocqueville Institute, June 2002). However, the computer security community has, if anything, a preference for open source for secure systems. See Ross Anderson, "Security in Open versus Closed Systems—The Dance of Boltzmann, Coase and Moore," and Roger Needham, "Security and Open Source," both papers presented at the conference "Open Source Software: Economics, Law and Policy," Institut de Economie Industrielle (IDEI), Toulouse, France, June 20–21, 2002 (www.idei.asso.fr/english/epresent/index.html [August 2002].)

45. The importance of this point has been raised recently by open source advocates at www.sincerechoice.com.

46. Paul Krugman, Competitiveness: An International Reader (New York: Foreign Affairs, 1994).

47. SourceForge lists numerous "me too" open source projects that are quite similar to already existing programs. Not surprisingly, few of these receive sustained support.

48. To obtain a patent, an invention is supposed to be nonobvious to a practitioner skilled in the relevant art. See Robert P. Merges, Patent Law and Policy: Cases and Materials, 2d ed. (Charlottesville, Va.: The Mitchie Company, 1997); Samuel Kortum and Josh Lerner, "What Is behind the Recent Surge in Patenting?" Research Policy, vol. 28, no. 1 (1999), pp. 1–22; Bronwyn H. Hall and Rosemary Ham Ziedonis, "The Patent Paradox Revisited: An Empirical Study of Patenting in the U.S. Semiconductor Industry, 1979–1995," RAND Journal of Economics, vol. 32, no. 1 (2001), pp. 101–28; Josh Lerner, "Patenting in the Shadow of Competitors," Journal of Law and Economics, vol. 38, no. 2 (1995), pp. 463–95; Glynn S. Lunney Jr., "E-Obviousness," Michigan Telecommunications and Technology Law Review, vol. 7 (Fall 2000–Spring 2001), p. 363.

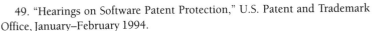

49. "Hearings on Software Patent Protection," U.S. Patent and Trademark Office, January–February 1994.

50. Jean Lanjouw and Mark Schankerman, "Enforcing Intellectual Property Rights," Working Paper 8656 (Cambridge, Mass.: National Bureau of Economic Research, December 2001).

51. Wesley M. Cohen, Richard R. Nelson, and John P. Walsh, "Protecting Their Intellectual Assets: Appropriability Conditions and Why U.S. Manufacturing Firms Patent (or Not)," Working Paper 7552 (Cambridge, Mass.: National Bureau of Economic Research, February 2000).

52. Only 51 percent of corporate patent portfolios were used according to Edwin Mansfield, The Economics of Technological Change (W. W. Norton, 1968), p. 207. Rossman and Sanders reported that only 31 percent were in use at the time of their survey, although about half were used at some time; see Joseph Rossman, and Barkev Sanders, "The Patent Utilization Study," Patent, Trade-Mark, and Copyright Journal of Research and Education, vol. 1, no. 1 (1957), pp. 74–111. And a 1998 study found that about 60 percent were used; see "Intellectual Property Rights Benchmark Study" (London: Business Planning and Research International, 1998), cited in "The Patent and License Exchange: Enabling a Global IP Marketplace," Harvard Business School Case Study N9-601-019 (July 17, 2000).

53. Peter C. Grindley and David J. Teece, "Managing Intellectual Capital: Licensing and Cross-Licensing in Semiconductors and Electronics," California Management Review, vol. 39, no. 2 (1997), pp. 8–41; Hall and Ziedonis, "Patent Paradox Revisited," pp. 101–28.

54. See, for example, Bruce Perens, "Preparing for the Intellectual-Property Offensive," LinuxWorld (www.linuxworld.com/linuxworld/lw-1998-11/lw-11-thesource.html [August 2002]); Karston M. Self, "Cooperative OSS Patent Pool—Proposal" (http://home.netcom.com/~kmself.osspatpool/index.html [August 2002]).

55. Quoted in Fred Warshofsky, The Patent Wars (Wiley, 1994), p. 170.

56. "IBM Public License Version 1.0" (http://oss.software.ibm.com/developerworks/opensource/license10.html [August 2002]).

57. See www.openpatents.org (August 2002).

58. There have been some notable examples, including a leading developer of free 3D software, Helmut Dersch. See Craig Bicknell, "Virtual Reality, Real Trouble," Wired News, July 20, 1999 (www.wired.com/news/ipo/0,1350,20824,00.html [August 2002]).

59. For information on patents, see www.uspto.gov/main/patents.htm (August 2002).

60. This declaration appears on a sign in the lobby of the U.S. Patent and Trademark Office. See also USPTO, "FY2001 Corporate Plan," 2000 (www.uspto.gov/web/offices/com/corpplan [August 2002]), which states, "The Patent Business is one of the PTO's three core businesses. The primary mission of the Patent Business is to help customers get patents." Brian Kahin provides a political

economic analysis of the USPTO in "The Expansion of the Patent System: Politics and Political Economy," *First Monday*, vol. 6, no. 1 (2001).

61. Cecil D. Quillen Jr. and Ogden H. Webster, "Continuing Patent Applications and Performance of the U.S. Patent Office," *Federal Circuit Bar Journal*, vol. 11, no. 1 (2001), pp. 1–21; Stuart Graham and others, "Post-Issue Patent 'Quality Control': A Comparative Study of US Patent Re-examinations and European Patent Oppositions," Working Paper 8807 (Cambridge, Mass.: National Bureau of Economic Research, February 2002).

62. See Adam B. Jaffe, "The U.S. Patent System in Transition: Policy Innovation and the Innovation Process," *Research Policy*, vol. 29, no. 4–5 (2000), pp. 531–57.

63. Lunney, "E-Obviousness."

64. Ibid. These figures are obtained by multiplying Lunney's data for figure 1 (Percentage of Patents Held Invalid Where Validity at Issue and Decided) by the data in figure 2 (Percentage of Invalid Patents Found Invalid for Obviousness).

65. U.S. Patent and Trademark Office, "Our Business: An Introduction to the PTO" (www.uspto.gov/web/menu/intro.html [August 2002]).

66. James Bessen and Eric S. Maskin, "Sequential Innovation, Patents and Imitation," Department of Economics Working Paper 00-01 (Massachusetts Institute of Technology, January 2000).

67. Grindley and Teece, "Managing Intellectual Capital."

68. This idea has been proposed by Jean-Paul Smets, "Stimulating Competition and Innovation in the Information Society" (www.pro-innovation.org/rapport_brevet/brevets_plan-en.pdf [August 2002]). Another approach is to make patent renewals much more expensive so that only truly important innovations would have long patent terms. See Francesca Cornelli and Mark Schankerman, "Patent Renewals and R&D Incentives," *RAND Journal of Economics*, vol. 30, no. 2 (1999), pp. 197–214. This, however, would work against open source developers.

69. Randall Davis and others, "A Manifesto Concerning the Legal Protection of Computer Programs," *Columbia Law Review*, vol. 94 (December 1994), p. 2318. The current term for patents is twenty years, while software is typically amortized over thirty months.

70. Currently, patent fees are lower for individuals. However, something more far-reaching is required to provide equal access since search costs and legal fees are typically expensive.

Chapter 3
Politics and Programming:
Government Preferences for Promoting
Open Source Software

1. For further details concerning governments that have or are considering policies to promote open source software, see David S. Evans and Bernard Reddy,

"Government Preferences for Promoting Open-Source Software: A Solution in Search of a Problem," working paper (Cambridge, Mass.: National Economic Research Associates, May 2002), also available at the Social Science Research Network website (http://papers.ssrn.com/sol3/papers.cfm?abstract_id=313202 [August 2002]). Open source software is distributed under very different terms than typical proprietary software. The source code is protected by copyright. However, it is distributed under a license that enables people to use the source code only if they comply with certain conditions. There are several different open source licenses, which are discussed in this chapter.

2. The returns to investment in software appear to be highly skewed. Josh Lerner, "Risk and the New Economy: Or Why, When Profits Are Good, They Should Be Very, Very Good," *Milken Institute Review*, 3d quarter (2001), p. 24.

3. "1993 Worldwide Software Review and Forecast," IDC Report 8324 (Framingham, Mass., December 1993), pp. 10–16, table 2; "Worldwide Software Market Forecast Summary, 2001–2005," IDC Report 25569 (September 2001), pp. 1–2, table 1, and pp. 164–65, table 16; Bruce T. Grimm and Robert P. Parker, "Recognition of Business and Government Expenditures for Software as Investment: Methodology and Quantitative Impacts, 1959–98," BEA Methodological Paper presented at the May 5, 2000, meeting of the Bureau of Economic Research Advisory Committee, Washington, D.C., and "2001 Annual NIPA Revision," Bureau of Economic Analysis and the U.S. Department of Justice, August 2001, tables 1 and 11.

4. Based on worldwide licensing of prepackaged software. See "1993 Worldwide Software Review," pp. 10–16, table 2; "Worldwide Software Market Forecast Summary, 2001–2005," pp. 1–2, table 1, and pp. 164–65, table 16.

5. Bureau of Labor Statistics and the Census Bureau, "Consumer Price Index—All Urban Consumers: Computer Software and Accessories," Series ID-CUUR0000SEEE02 (Department of Commerce, March 20, 2002).

6. Standard and Poor's COMPUSTAT Data, 1985–2000. Software firms are those that report their primary SIC code to be 7372 (software publishers).

7. Data purchased from Delphion (www.delphion.com [August 2002]). Some commentators have argued that it should not be possible to patent software. See Lawrence Lessig, *The Future of Ideas* (Random House, 2001), pp. 205–17. See subsequent discussion.

8. "Worldwide Software Market Forecast Summary, 2001–2005," pp. 27–29, table 2. Figures based on worldwide packaged software revenue. This report provides firm-level data only for the 100 largest software vendors, covering 61 percent of packaged software. Firms ranked 80th to 100th largest each hold 1 percent of the market. For purposes of this calculation, we assume that the remaining 39 percent of the market is composed of similar firms whose market shares also equal 1 percent (an assumption that produces the highest possible HHI estimate). The Antitrust Division of the U.S. Department of Justice and the Federal Trade Commission consider industries with HHIs of less than 1,000 to be competitive and those with HHIs of 1,800 or greater to be

cause for "significant competitive concerns." Department of Justice and Federal Trade Commission, "Concentration and Market Shares,"*1992 Horizontal Merger Guidelines* (revised April 8, 1997), section 1.5 (www.usdoj.gov/atr/public/guidelines/horiz_book/hmgl.html [April 1, 2002]). As a practical matter, an HHI under 2,000 is seldom a serious concern for the U.S. antitrust enforcement agencies.

9. Bureau of the Census, "1997 Economic Census, Concentration Ratios in Manufacturing" (www.census.gov/prod/ec97/ms31s-cr.pdf [May 20, 2002]). Figures are based upon industries categorized at the four-digit SIC industry level. The simple average is reported above; the revenue-weighted average is equal to 462, and the median is equal to 282.

10. "1993 Worldwide Software Review," pp. 10–16, table 2, and "Worldwide Software Market Forecast Summary, 2001–2005," pp. 27–29, table 2.

11. IMS Health, "M&A Drives Decade of Change," April 25, 2001 (www.imsglobal.com/insight/news_story/0104/news_story_010425.htm [April 1, 2002], citing *World Review*, 1990–2000).

12. David S. Evans and Richard Schmalensee, "Some Economic Aspects of Antitrust Analysis in Dynamically Competitive Industries," in Adam B. Jaffe, Josh Lerner, and Scott Stern, eds., *Innovation Policy and the Economy*, vol. 2 (MIT Press, 2002), pp. 1–49.

13. "Worldwide Software Market Forecast Summary, 2001–2005," pp. 27–29, table 2.

14. The government already plays some role in the software industry by sponsoring research and development of software through universities and government research laboratories. This chapter does not address the issue of whether such research and development support for software is good public policy. It does, however, address the issue of whether research and development support for GPL software is good public policy. See subsequent discussion.

15. Joe Wilcox, "IBM to Spend $1 Billion on Linux in 2001," *CNET*, December 12, 2000 (www.news.com.com/2100-1001-249750.html?tag=mainstry [May 23, 2002]).

16. See www.apple.com/macosx/technologies/darwin.html (May 23, 2002); www.windriver.com/products/html/free_bsd.html (May 23, 2002); www.freebsd.org/gallery/cgallery.html (May 23, 2002).

17. See "BSD a Better OS Than Linux?" *ZDNet*, July 21, 1999 (http://zdnet.com.com/2100-11-501149.html?legacy=zdnn [May 23, 2002]); also see "Kirk McKusick, Part 1" (www.sendmail.net/interviews/interview004.shtml [May 23, 2002]).

18. There is some controversy over how closely software must be intertwined with GPL software to be covered by this provision. See Evans and Reddy, "Government Preferences for Promoting Open-Source Software."

19. Free Software Foundation, "The GNU GPL and the American Way" (www.gnu.org/philosophy/gpl-american-way.html [April 2, 2002]).

20. Apache is a web server; Sendmail is a mail server; BIND is an implementation of the Domain Name System (DNS) protocols.

21. "Ximian-Led Mono Project Selects New Flexible Licensing Model in Move Lauded by Industry Leaders Intel and HP," press release, January 28, 2002 (www.ximian.com/about_us/press_center/press_releases/mono_partners.html [May 22, 2002]).

22. Ibid.

23. This is based on an analysis of 25,194 projects listed on SourceForge, a website that provides free hosting services to open source projects. For further details, see Evans and Reddy, "Government Preferences for Promoting Open-Source Software."

24. See Annalee Newitz, "A Brief History of Linux," *The Standard*, February 14, 2000 (www.thestandard.com/article/0,1902,9457,00.html [May 12, 2002]).

25. Among the more significant open source software products are operating systems, such as Linux (which is much more popular on computers for servers than for end-users), distributed under the GPL; databases, such as MySQL, distributed under the GPL; Samba, GPL software that allows servers running Linux and other Unix-like operating systems to emulate Windows servers; e-mail servers, such as BSD-based Sendmail; web servers, such as BSD-based Apache; implementation of the Domain Name System protocols, such as BSD-based BIND; implementation of a windowing system, such as BSD-based Xfree86; and scripting languages, such as BSD-based Perl. Linux also successfully operates on handheld computers and embedded devices, such as cell phones and web phones, TV set-top boxes, web pads, Internet radios, audio systems, and PDAs. See Linda Musthaler, "Open Source Handheld Computers," *Network World*, February 12, 2001 (www.itworld.com/appdev/356/nww00408511/ [May 23, 2002]). See also "The Embedded Linux 'Cool Devices' Quick Reference Guide," January 24, 2002 (www.linuxdevices.com/articles/at4936596231.html [May 23, 2002]).

26. Eric Steven Raymond, "Global Implications of the Reputation Game Model," in *Homesteading the Noosphere* (www.tuxedo.org/~esr/writings/homesteading/homesteading/ar01s12.html [August 2002]).

27. Brian Behlendorf, "Open Source as a Business Strategy," in Chris DiBona, Sam Ockman, and Mark Stone, eds., *Open Sources: Voices from the Open Source Revolution* (Sebastopol, Calif.: O'Reilly and Associates, January 1999), p. 159.

28. A recent review of StarOffice—an open source clone of Microsoft Office—by the *Wall Street Journal* noted that, in comparison to Microsoft Office, StarOffice is "harder to use, less intuitive." Walter Mossberg, "Too Bad; StarOffice Is Weak Competition for Microsoft Office," *Wall Street Journal*, May 16, 2002, p. B1.

29. For someone who seems to take this approach, see Lawrence Lessig, "Open Code and Open Societies," keynote address presented at Free Software—A Model for Society, Tutzing, Germany, June 1, 2000 (http://cyberlaw.stanford.edu/lessig/content/articles/works/opensocd1.pdf [May 23, 2002]).

30. Newitz, "A Brief History of Linux."

31. See description of OpenOffice at www.cybersite.com.au/home/home.html (May 23, 2002).

32. For example, see Red Hat, Inc., Form 10-K for the fiscal year ended February 28, 2001.

33. John Viega, "The Myth of Open Source Security" (www.earthweb.com/article/0,,10455_626641_1,00.html [May 23, 2002]); Richard Stiennon and John Pescatore, "No Software Will Ever Be Totally Secure," March 21, 2002 (http://techupdate.zdnet.com/techupdate/stories/main/0,14179,5105156,00.html [May 23, 2002]).

34. In July 2001, the City Council of Florence passed a motion on the open source preference in the public administration. The motion was introduced by Green Party member Alessio Papini. See www.interlex.com/pa/firenze.htm (Italian; May 23, 2002).

35. See www.heute.t-online.de/zdfheute/artikel/0,1251,comp-0-178943,00.html (German; May 23, 2002).

36. Joseph E. Stiglitz, *Principles of Microeconomics* (W. W. Norton, 1997), p. 163.

37. Lessig, *The Future of Ideas.*

38. See, for example, Lawrence Lessig, "Code and the Commons," February 9, 1999 (http://cyberlaw.stanford.edu/lessig/content/articles/works/fordham.pdf [April 24, 2002]); and "May the Source Be with You," *Wired*, December 2001 (www.wired.com/wired/archive/9.12/lessig_pr.html [April 24, 2002]).

39. One might argue that price competition between two firms would offset the loss of scale economies and result in lower prices on net. However, if that were the case, a second provider could enter the market and compete price down without government assistance.

40. For example, see Carl Shapiro and Hal R. Varian, *Information Rules: A Strategic Guide to the Network Economy* (Harvard Business School Press, 1999), pp. 300–02, 311–15.

41. Governments do not have a good track record of trying to centrally manage economies. For further details, see Evans and Reddy, "Government Preferences for Promoting Open-Source Software."

42. For example, see Dennis W. Carlton and Jeffrey M. Perloff, *Modern Industrial Organization*, 3d ed. (Reading, Mass.: Addison-Wesley, 2000), pp. 505–07.

43. There seems to be no economic justification for this support of the GPL. In addition, it is inconsistent with government policy in other areas, where universities and government research laboratories have been encouraged over the past twenty years to spin off research into commercial products, particularly through the licensing of patents that emerge from their research. There are many examples of government research released under the GPL. For example, the Beowulf clustering software for Linux, released under the GPL, was originally developed by NASA. More advanced clustering software was developed at Sandia National Laboratories, also released under the GPL. The next version of

the Reiser File System is sponsored primarily by the Defense Advanced Research Projects Agency (DARPA) and will be licensed under the GPL. For further details, see Evans and Reddy, "Government Preferences for Promoting Open-Source Software."

44. For example, the Patent and Trademark Law Amendments Act (also known as the Bayh-Dole Act) of 1980 encouraged universities and small businesses to commercialize inventions by permitting exclusive licensing of intellectual property that was developed with public funding. In exchange for the right to elect title to an invention, the licensor must agree to properly manage the invention and provide reports to the government. Since the passage of Bayh-Dole, universities have increasingly set up technology transfer programs and actively patented and commercialized inventions. See Council of Government Relations, "The Bayh-Dole Act: A Guide to the Law and Implementing Regulations," September 1999 (www.cogr.edu/bayh-dole.htm [May 20, 2002]).

45. For further discussion, see Evans and Reddy, "Government Preferences for Promoting Open-Source Software."

46. See presentation by James Bessen at the AEI-Brookings Joint Center for Regulatory Studies Conference "Is Open Source the Future of Software?" Washington, D.C., April 12, 2002.

Chapter 4
Open Source Baselines:
Compared to What?

1. For example, Craig Mundie argues that General Public License software—as distinct from open source software—may lead to the "forking" of the code base (hence causing incompatibility), weakened interoperability, product instability, problematic strategic planning for business leaders, and the risk of forcing intellectual property into the public domain. Craig Mundie, "The Commercial Software Model," remarks at the Stern School of Business, New York University (www.microsoft.com/presspass/exec/craig/05-03sharedsource.asp [August 2002]).

2. "In the heat of their Hatfield-McCoy feud, Microsoft and Netscape have taken HTML hostage. Each company is proposing incompatible ways to extend the Web's lingua franca, exposing us to the danger that we'll soon have two different dialects." See Jesse Berst, "Microsoft, Netscape Feud Puts HTML's Future at Risk," April 11, 1997 (www.zdnet.com/anchordesk/story/story_827.html [August 2002]).

3. See Richard Stallman, "What Is Copyleft?" (www.fsf.org/copyleft/copyleft.html [August 2002]); Teresa Hill, "Fragmenting the Copyleft Movement: The Public Will Not Prevail," *Utah Law Review* (1999), p. 797.

4. See generally Richard Stallman, "Linux and the GNU Project" (www.gnu.org/gnu/linux-and-gnu.html [August 2002]).

5. There is an important quibble about what "modifies" means. The Free Software Foundation sometimes seems to suggest that any change in GPL-covered code would be a derivative work, thereby subject to copyright regulation. For a discussion of the derivation of subsequent distribution of a modified work as a form of original work versus the derivative work itself, see David McGowan, "Legal Implications of Open-Source Software," *Illinois Law Review* (2001), p. 254.

6. See, for example, Bjørn Reese and Daniel Stenberg, "Working without Copyleft," December 19, 2001 (www.oreillynet.com/pub/a/policy/2001/12/12/transition.html [August 2002]). The authors explain their feelings of repulsion for the GPL because, in its fear of corporate exploitation, it is uncooperative and has an overly extensive scope that becomes a deterrent to development.

7. "Apache soon became the number one server in the world. To this day, two-thirds of the servers on the World Wide Web are Apache servers." Lawrence Lessig, *The Future of Ideas* (Random House, 2001), pp. 55–56. See also David A. Wheeler, "Why Open Source Software/Free Software? Look at the Numbers!" (www.dwheeler.com/oss_fs_why.html [August 2002]).

8. "Source code is the code that programmers write. It is close to a natural language, but not quite a natural language. A program is written in source code, but to be run it must be converted into a language the machine can read. Some source code is converted on the fly—BASIC, for example, is usually interpreted by the computer as the computer runs a BASIC program. But most source code—or the most powerful source code—is 'compiled' before it is run. The computer converts the source code into either assembly code (which mavens can read) or object code (which only geniuses and machines can read). Object code is machine-readable. It is an undifferentiated string of 0s and 1s that instructs the machine about the tasks it is to perform. Programmers do not directly write object code, even if some are able to decipher it; programmers write source code. Object code speaks to the computer; source code speaks to humans and to computers (compilers); assembly code speaks to mavens and computers." See Lawrence Lessig, *Code and Other Laws of Cyberspace* (Basic Books, 1999), p. 103.

9. For a general introduction to public goods, see the discussion of common pool resources in Elinor Ostrom, *Governing the Commons: The Evolution of Institutions for Collective Action* (Cambridge University Press, 1990). She explores the nonexcludable nature of public goods via the thought-experiment of the grazing field "open to all," allowing unfettered access to all interested grazers (pp. 2–3). She also explains that, even in scenarios where excludability may be achieved, it is nevertheless practically impossible, since the costs of excluding others are prohibitive (pp. 30–33). As to the nonrivalrous nature of public goods, see Ostrom (p. 30) for a brief introduction to the notion of practically nonrivalrous public goods (allowance for maximal allocation of goods with no significant depletion of those goods for others), and see Lessig, *Future of Ideas*, pp. 20–23. (Language, for example, is a perfectly nonrivalrous public good, since your use of it doesn't impede mine.)

10. Ostrom, *Governing the Commons*, chap. 3. As Ostrom demonstrates, it doesn't follow that every public good requires state intervention for it to be supplied. Nor does it follow that every public good needs to be "privatized" for it to be supplied.

11. According to Yochai Benkler, "A commons-based information policy relies on the observation that some resources that serve as inputs for information production and exchange have economic or technological characteristics that make them susceptible to be allocated without requiring that any single organization, regulatory agency or property owner, clear conflicting uses of the resource. For example, the nonrivalrous nature of information, and the perfect renewability of radio frequency spectrum, create the possibility of sustainable commons in information used as an input into new information production, and in the RF spectrum, respectively." Benkler, "The Commons as a Neglected Factor of Information Policy," paper presented at the Twenty-sixth Annual Telecommunications Policy Research Conference, Alexandria, Va., October 1998 (www.law.nyu.edu/benklery/ [August 2002]). James Boyle describes the emerging quandary of how to entice development and creativity of information in the context of increasingly "free, complete, instantaneous, and universally available . . . information flows that are costless, general, and fast." Boyle, *Shamans, Software, and Spleens* (Harvard University Press, 1996), p. 35. David McGowan notes that "the low cost of copying and using code combined with the broad grants of the relevant licenses creates a situation that resembles a commons in some respects." McGowan, "Legal Implications," p. 244.

According to the UN secretary general's *Millennium Report* (p. 159): "[T]he core product in this sector—information—has unique attributes, not shared by others. The steel used to construct a building, or the boots worn by the workers constructing it, cannot be consumed by anyone else. Information is different. Not only is it available for multiple uses and users, it becomes more valuable the more it is used. The same is true of the networks that link up different sources of information." Reprinted in "Information as Global Public Good: A Right to Knowledge and Communication," Oxfam International Campaign Proposal 2000 (http://danny.oz.au/free-software/advocacy/oicampaign.html [August 2002]). From the viewpoint of one venture capitalist, "Put simply, in a world where there are essentially no costs to replicate content and it is effectively impossible to stop anyone from doing so at will, the current economic model underpinning content creation [including code writing] will be dead." See Dan Kohn, "Content Is a Pure Public Good" (http://db.tidbits.com/getbits.acgi?tbart=06604 [August 2002]). Finally, writing for the UN Food and Agriculture Organization, Bernard Woods advocates the transformation of digital technologies, including software and other facilitative technologies, from potential public goods into public goods in an almost traditional sense, that is, provided and guaranteed by governmental entities in a manner similar to utilities or a lighthouse. "A Public Good, a Private Responsibility" (www.fao.org/waicent/faoinfo/sustdev/dodirect/doengb02.htm [August 2002]).

12. See William M. Landes and Richard A. Posner, "An Economic Analysis of Copyright Law," *Journal of Legal Studies*, vol. 18, no. 2 (1989), pp. 325–63. Landes and Posner put forth an economic analysis of how the law may facilitate the maximally efficient design and enforcement of copyright law, stipulating that "for copyright law to promote economic efficiency, its principal legal doctrines must, at least approximately, maximize the benefits from creating additional works minus both the losses from limiting access and the costs of administering copyright protection."

13. See Kenneth J. Arrow, "Economic Welfare and the Allocation of Resources for Invention," in Richard R. Nelson, ed., *The Rate and Direction of Inventive Activity* (National Bureau of Economic Research and Princeton University Press, 1962), p. 609. For a more recent discussion of Arrow's analysis, see Gillian K. Hadfield, "The Economics of Copyright: An Historical Perspective," *ASCAP Copyright Law Symposium*, no. 38 (1992), pp. 39–40. Hadfield states that "when a resource is indivisible, the marginal cost of increasing the quantity available is zero; optimal allocation therefore requires that it be distributed at a price of zero. Yet clearly if price equals zero, then the fixed cost of producing the resource will not be covered by the market. . . . As in the case of ordinary public goods, information is underproduced to the extent that price is reduced to zero away from the average cost of its production."

14. However, tools to defeat some of the public goods aspects of software cannot eliminate them. There is certainly plenty of software piracy, despite the mix of public and private tools to protect against improper use.

15. "Once the work is created, the author's efforts can be incorporated into another copy virtually without cost." See Landes and Posner, "An Economic Analysis," p. 327.

16. This does not mean that there is always, or even often, a line dividing the necessary from the not. But where there has been protection sufficient to induce the production of a certain good, at least the terms of that protection should not be extended. See brief of "17 Economists" as amici curiae in support of petitioners to the Supreme Court of the United States, *Eldred* v. *Ashcroft* (www.eldred.cc/legal/supremecourt.html [August 2002]).

17. Most of the commentary on free and open source software has been "focused on explaining the rationale behind growing participation in this movement." See Siobhan Clare O'Mahony, "The Emergence of a New Commercial Actor," Ph.D. dissertation, Stanford University, 2002, p. 52, citing Josh Lerner and Jean Tirole, "The Simple Economics of Open Source," Working Paper W7600 (Cambridge, Mass.: National Bureau of Economic Research, 2002). See also Justin Pappas Johnson, "Economics of Open Source Software," working paper, May 17, 2001 (http://opensource.mit.edu/papers/johnsonopensource.pdf [August 2002]).

18. As William Baumol writes, "Individuals who have invested directly or indirectly in the economy's innovation processes can be estimated, conservatively, to obtain less than 10% of the total economic benefits contributed by new technology and new products." Baumol, "Pareto Optimal Sizes of Innovation

Spillovers" (www.econ.nyu.edu/user/baumolw/inovspi1.htm [August 2002]). Baumol's work is consistent with the extensive research of Eric von Hippel tracking the source of innovation in a wide range of contexts. As von Hippel has demonstrated, there are many contexts beyond software where innovation is provided by innovators who do not recover the value of the innovation. See Eric von Hippel, "Horizontal Innovation Networks—by and for Users" (http://opensource.mit.edu/papers/vonhippel3.pdf [August 2002]).

19. According to their websites, Peet's Coffee opened in Berkeley in 1966, while Starbucks opened in Seattle in 1971.

20. For a more skeptical view of this comparison, see Mathias Strasser, "A New Paradigm in Intellectual Property Law? The Case against Open Sources," *Stanford Technology Law Review* (2001), p. 4, para. 80.

21. See Carolyn Elefant, "Do Not Copy That Brief," *Legal Times Intellectual Property Magazine*, May 7, 2001 (www.his.com/~israel/loce/press.html [August 2002]). Elefant argues that although legal briefs appear to satisfy the criteria traditionally demanded of copyrightable material (such as originality, inclusion in statutorily identified categories of the Copyright Act, fixation in tangible medium), whether lawyers may expect or should want briefs to be copyrightable is due further thought. For example, she argues that even if they are copyrightable, there are massive enforcement hurdles, and tightening of access to briefs may damage research interests and decrease quality of legal briefs.

22. "Conventional markets work very well where the commodities are well defined, where the demand and the nature of the customer's need are well defined, and where the property rights or contractual relationships are well defined. But software is not typically a standardized commodity. Packaged software has never represented as much of a third of all software investment in the United States. Open source is thus in some sense a better business model because it's easier to customize." James Bessen, remarks at the AEI-Brookings Joint Center for Regulatory Studies conference "Is Open Source the Future of Software?" April 12, 2002 (www.aei.brookings.org/events/page.php?id=59#bessen).

23. Baumol, "Pareto Optimal Sizes of Innovation Spillovers."

24. See www.linuxlinks.com/embedded/.

25. For a brief summary, see David S. Evans, "Is Free Software the Wave of the Future?" *Milken Institute Review*, 4th quarter (2001), pp. 38–39. The most significant reason for commercial entities to support open or free software projects is that they keep the cost of complements low. IBM sells hardware; if it can keep the cost of operating systems low, that will increase the demand for its hardware. See Lessig, *Future*, pp. 69–70.

26. See James Bessen, "Open Source Software: Free Provision of Complex Public Goods," ROI Working Paper, July 2002 (www.researchoninnovation.org/online.htm). For the argument that peer pressure increases quality in open systems, see Harlan D. Mills, "Top-down Programming in Large Systems," in Randall Rustin, ed., *Debugging Techniques in Large Systems* (Englewood Cliffs, N.J.: Prentice Hall, 1971).

27. My argument is consistent with a point long made by Eric von Hippel: firms that give users the opportunity to innovate upon their product do better in the market than those that do not. This gives firms a reason to support a kind of open source development, and this open source development is supported by innovators who never capture the full value of their innovation. See Eric von Hippel, "Customers as Innovators: A New Way to Create Value," *Harvard Business Review*, vol. 80, no. 4 (2002), p. 74.

28. For details on French policy, see "France towards Open e-Government— Government Agency to Enforce Open Standards and Promote Open Source/ Free Software," November 21, 2001 (http://old.lwn.net/2001/1129/pr/ pr4501.php3 [August 2002]). On Germany, see David McHugh, "German Government Signs Deal With IBM," AP Wire Service, June 3, 2002 (www.radicus.net/ news/wed/cx/agermany-linux.rb-t_cu3.asp). On China, see Andy Tai, "Taiwan to Start National Plan to Push Free Software," June 3, 2002 (www.kuro5hin.org/ story/2002/6/3/55433/41738 [August 2002]).

29. See David S. Evans and Bernard Reddy, "Government Preferences for Promoting Open-Source Software: A Solution in Search of a Problem," working paper (Cambridge, Mass.: National Economic Research Associates, May 21, 2002) (http://ssrn.com/abstract_id=313202 [August 2002]). This paper is a careful and extraordinarily complete analysis of the issue. While it asserts that I have argued that open source and free software is "innovative" (p. 64), in fact I have not made any claim about whether the software itself is innovative. My claim is that the platform it helped build produced innovation. Evans and Reddy collect a wide range of reasons why the government might, from an economic perspective, prefer open source or free software. They have not included the reasons provided here.

30. Mundie, "The Commercial Software Model."

31. "With respect to procurement, I would run the government like a business." See David Evans, remarks at the AEI-Brookings Joint Center for Regulatory Studies conference "Is Open Source the Future of Software?" April 12, 2002 (www.aei.brookings.org/events/page.php?id=59#evans).

32. Mundie, "The Commercial Software Model." Microsoft makes an independent point about the potential "danger" of GPL licensed for other intellectual property owned by the software developer. See also www.microsoft.com/ sharedsource.

33. Evans and Reddy make a similar argument against the government funding GPL-covered software. Evans and Reddy, "Government Preferences," pp. 74–76. They note that the government has traditionally funded research that either goes into the public domain or is used by the military or is spun off for commercial purposes (p. 75). But when the government funds research that produces GPL-covered software, Evans and Reddy contend that "there is no economic justification for this support of the GPL." Their argument is in essence that "support of GPL projects is incompatible with commercial spin-off efforts, since the GPL is incompatible with proprietary, commercial software" (p. 76).

There are many unstated assumptions built into this argument. First, to say that the GPL is "incompatible with proprietary, commercial software" is not to say it is "incompatible with commercial spin-off efforts." There are plenty of commercial firms that develop and support GPL software—IBM to name just one. No doubt GPL-covered code is not a resource for "proprietary, commercial software" development, to the extent that development modifies and redistributes GPL-covered code. But again, there is plenty of proprietary, commercial software development that need not modify and redistribute GPL-covered code, such as GNU/Linux, just as there is plenty of proprietary, commercial software development that need not modify and redistribute Windows XP.

Second, this argument takes the commercialization of government-funded research as the baseline and measures "economic justification" against that. But there is no argument for this baseline. Certainly the government funds lots of research that passes into the public domain. Evans and Reddy have not provided an argument against that. To the extent innovation passes into the public domain, it may or may not be less exploitable by commercial entities. It was a concern about a lack of incentives to exploit resources that lead to the passage of the Bayh-Dole Act, permitting the patenting of government-funded research. The effect of that act on research has been extremely controversial; for example, see Arti Kaur Rai, "Regulating Scientific Research: Intellectual Property Rights and the Norms of Science," *Northwestern University Law Review*, vol. 94 (1999), pp. 136–37. But unless there is some reason to reject supporting research for the public domain, there cannot be a general, economic reason to reject supporting research for the GPL. The only general argument is the one Microsoft seems to be making. But this again would apply to government support of proprietary software development as much as government support of GPL software development.

34. See Lessig, *Future*, pp. 206–14.

Chapter 5
The Future of Software:
Enabling the Marketplace to Decide

1. Although these views are often associated with the Free Software Foundation and its founder, Richard Stallman, strands of this thinking can be found throughout the open source community.

2. This topic is discussed in more detail in a subsequent section. "GNU" is a recursive acronym that stands for "GNU's Not UNIX." The acronym reflects the original purpose of the GNU Project, which was to develop a "free" alternative to the UNIX operating system. See Richard Stallman, *The GNU Project* (www.gnu.org [2002]).

3. For a description of the BSD license and similar licenses as "permissive," see Sean Doherty, "The Law and Open Source Software," *Network Computing*, October 29, 2001.

4. Ibid., describing GPL and similar licenses as "more restrictive" than the BSD license.

5. As Brian Behlendorf, a leading open source developer, has noted, "[The GPL's] 'viral' behavior has been trumpeted widely by open-source advocates as a way to ensure that code that begins free remains free—that there is no chance of a commercial interest forking their own development version from the available code and committing resources that are not made public." Brian Behlendorf, "Open Source as a Business Strategy," in Chris DiBona, Sam Ockman, and Mark Stone, eds., *Open Sources: Voices from the Open Source Revolution* (Sebastopol, Calif.: O'Reilly and Associates, 1999), p. 167.

6. Bureau of Economic Analysis, *Recognition of Business and Government Expenditures for Software as Investment: Methodology and Quantitative Impacts, 1959–98* (Department of Commerce, 2000), pp. 28, 32–36. This report concludes that for the period 1959 through 1998, "prices for prepackaged software have fallen sharply" (p. 6).

7. Business Software Alliance, *Opportunities and Growth: A Vision for the Future, 2001–2005* (Washington, 2000), p. 6.

8. Ibid., pp. 8–9.

9. PricewaterhouseCoopers, *Contributions of the Packaged Software Industry to the Global Economy* (New York, 1999), p. 10.

10. Tim Reason, "Linux: When Free Isn't," September 1, 2001 (www.cfo.com/article/1,5309,48186,00.html [August 2002]).

11. See Microsoft Corporation, *The Microsoft Shared Source Philosophy,* 2002 (www.microsoft.com/licensing/sharedsource).

12. See Department of Commerce, *Digital Economy 2000* (2000), p. 31.

13. Ibid., p. 3, note 5.

14. Some open source advocates also argue that innovation might better be served by curtailing or even eliminating IP rights in software. For example, see Lawrence Lessig, *The Future of Ideas: The Fate of the Commons in a Connected World* (Random House, 2001), pp. 250–53, 255–59 (arguing, among other things, for shorter and less robust copyright protection for software). Yet, just as legal protection for real and personal property is a necessary prerequisite for a market in land and goods, legal protection for intellectual property is a necessary precondition for a market in intangible goods. The marketplace is the single most important driver of software innovation. The primary impact of curtailing IP rights in software would be to distort or even destroy this marketplace, neither of which would promote innovation or consumer welfare.

15. See Microsoft Corporation, *Creating a Vibrant Information Technology Sector: Growth, Opportunity and Partnership* (Redmond, Wash., 2002), p. 12.

16. Ibid., p. 13.

17. Ibid., pp. 16, 20–21 (summarizing IDC data).

18. None of the studies cited in this section distinguish in their analyses between commercial and open source software firms. However, given that open source firms represent a relatively small share of revenue and employment in

the software sector, and that most open source firms are located in developed nations, the present economic impact of the open source software industry on developing nations is presumably negligible.

19. Microsoft, *Creating*, p. 16.

20. PricewaterhouseCoopers, *Contributions,* p. 10.

21. Oxford Analytica, *India: National IT Development: Explaining Success* (Redmond, Wash.: Microsoft, 2002) p. 1 (www.microsoft.com/presspass/events/glc02/docs/indiacs.doc [April 25, 2002]).

22. Microsoft, *Creating*, p. 21.

23. Ibid., pp. 17, 19.

24. For example, Marco Iansiti and Josh Lerner found that "compared to articles published by other institutions in 1996, a higher percentage of Microsoft publications were cited by other academic works, Microsoft publications had the highest average number of citations per cited paper, and they had the highest maximum number of citations per paper." Marco Iansiti and Josh Lerner, *Evidence Regarding Microsoft and Innovation* (Cambridge, Mass.: National Economic Research Associates, 2002), p. 9

25. In the past four years, Microsoft has made nineteen submissions to the W3C, sixteen of which were contributed under royalty-free terms.

26. J. D. Hildebrand, "Open Source Watch: Does Open Source Still Matter?" March 1, 2001 (www.sdtimes.com/cols/opensourcewatch_025.htm [August 2002]).

27. "There is evidence to support the notion that Windows-based systems enjoy a lower TCO [than Linux-based systems]. User, administrator and developer training are plentiful and cheap for Windows. Device support is much better, so Windows users have a wider range of hardware and peripherals from which to choose. Initial setup is simpler and less expensive. All of these factors . . . could make an investment in Windows more cost-effective than an investment in Linux." J. D. Hildebrand, "Open Source Watch: Proving Open Source Still Matters," April 1, 2001 (www.sdtimes.com/cols/opensourcewatch_027.htm [August 2002]).

28. Meta Group, "Commentary: Making the Move to Linux," August 31, 2001 (http://news.com.com/2009-1001-272500.html?legacy=cnet [August 2002]).

Contributors

James Bessen
Research on Innovation

David S. Evans
National Economic Research Associates

Robert W. Hahn
AEI-Brookings Joint Center for Regulatory Studies

Lawrence Lessig
Stanford University

Bradford L. Smith
Microsoft Corporation

Index

J O I N T   C E N T E R

AEI-BROOKINGS JOINT CENTER FOR REGULATORY STUDIES